ADMINISTR

James F. Nyquist

INTERNATIONAL FELLOWSHIP OF EVANGELICAL STUDENTS

HARROW·ENGLAND

© 1994 by IFES. Published by International Fellowship of Evangelical Students.

ISBN   1 899464 21

British Library Cataloguing in Publication Data
A catalogue record for this book is available from the British Library.

The International Fellowship of International Students is an association of national Christian movements in about 100 countries around the world. IFES Regional Secretaries who are located on each continent may be contacted through the Harrow office at the above address.

Telephone 081 863 8688; fax 081 863 8229.

Printed in the United States of America.

15	14	13	12	11	10	9	8	7	6	5	4	3	2	1
06	05	04	03	02	01	00	99	98	97	96	95	94		

PREFACE

INTRODUCTION

LEADING THE FELLOWSHIP

PEOPLE: OUR MOST VALUABLE RESOURCE

FUNDING THE WORK

PREFACE

I am delighted to commend this booklet to you. It is the mature fruit of Jim Nyquist's lifetime of service within InterVarsity USA and latterly with the International Fellowship of Evangelical Students. Several years ago my predecessor, Chua Wee Hian, had the idea of inviting Jim to use his writing and editorial skills to provide bite-sized contributions for leaders in our various member movements on key issues such as graduate work, building a team, fundraising, etc. The response to these short bulletins was so positive that we felt it would be worthwhile to write the material up more fully and make it more widely available. For two reasons I am delighted that Jim has been able to do this.

Firstly, Jim is a treasured and honored elder statesman in IFES. His friendship, gentle encouragement and wisdom have been deeply appreciated by many over the years within the Fellowship. Having this material compiled in a book provides a means of sharing the wisdom which God has given him with a wider readership.

Secondly, IFES has been known through the years both for its emphasis on partnership between its member movements and its emphasis on pioneering. I have found that a danger for many of our member movements in the pioneering stage is that they are so consumed with the task in hand of getting the work off the ground and the work of evangelism and discipleship that there is little interest in providing for the supportive structures which are needed for the work to mature and grow beyond the pioneering stage. It is particularly with the needs of these younger movements in mind that we commissioned this book. At the same time there are so many wise nuggets within the pages of the volume that even leaders who have been involved in student work for many years may profitably read the material and still perhaps be reminded of some crucial principles which they have forgotten.

I therefore warmly commend this book to you, and am sure that careful reading alone or discussion in groups will lead to God being honored as you serve Him.

Lindsay Brown
General Secretary
June 1993

INTRODUCTION

Since its founding in 1947, IFES has never swerved from its vision to establish indigenous student movements in every nation around the globe. With officially-recognized national movements in more than 90 countries, the IFES operates in a rich variety of language, cultural and socio-political environments.

Although students are the front-line workers, their effectiveness is enhanced greatly by the supporting team of voluntary and paid staff workers who in turn are enabled by a council/board of friends. It is for this supporting team of senior staff and council members that this book is written.

Because IFES Encourages each movement to identify with its own national ethos, the guidelines for membership are largely confined to Biblical and academic parameters. The *IFES Distinctives* reproduced below serve as a helpful overview of the context in which this book has been written. They merit frequent review.

I also commend to you Peter Lowman's history of IFES called *The Day of His Power* which should be available in the library of the national office of your own movement as well as IFES headquarters.

May God the Holy Spirit give you skill in blending the suggestions in this book with the grace of our Lord Jesus Christ and the characteristics of your nation as you serve students together.

James F. Nyquist
Downers Grove, Illinois
September, 1993

IFES DISTINCTIVES

IFES is an international, interdenominational FELLOWSHIP of national movements. While it recognizes the value of appropriate structures, it expresses its nature as a worldwide fellowship primarily through its network of relationships, investing in people more than in buildings, projects and programs, and recognizing its dependence upon God in prayer for growth and fruitfulness.

WE are an EVANGELICAL movement, acknowledging and seeking to submit to the LORDSHIP of Christ in every aspect of life and thought, committed to His gospel and to the authoritative Scriptures as foundational to all life and ministry. We stress the importance of personal devotional life, group Bible study and biblically-based evangelism and are committed to broad and deep theological reflection and action.

IN our understanding of LEADERSHIP and MINISTRY, we seek to follow the pattern of sacrificial, servant leadership of our Lord. We believe in participatory team structures, partnership between students and staff, and the importance of exercising spiritual influence through relationship and by example.

Recognizing our equality and oneness in Christ, we believe in national, contextualized and decentralized leadership, and are flexible in our methodology of ministry.

A SPECIAL DISTINCTIVE is our commitment to STUDENT LEADERSHIP on the campus, which is our main sphere of operation.

OUR MAIN OBJECTIVES are EVANGELISM, DISCIPLESHIP AND MISSION (understood holistically as embracing both the proclamation of the gospel and commitment to its social implications) among students and by students, in partnership with staff, graduates and faculty.

Our original vision to pioneer student work on unreached campuses and to establish evangelical student movements in every country of the world remains strong. That vision extends to the building of God's church worldwide as Christian students graduate and go on, by His grace, to serve in the church, in academic life and in the marketplace as "salt and light".

1
THE VALUE OF A PURPOSE STATEMENT

One of the simplest and most important "tools" available to a General Secretary (and a board/council as well) is a clearly defined statement of purpose. Such a statement will be used both consciously and unconsciously in daily decision-making, in recruiting personnel, in sifting options, in establishing priorities, and in providing clear leadership to the entire organization.

The most helpful purpose statements are not long, involved statements that try to include every detail. Rather they are most useful when they define the overall direction and objectives of the movement in a simple fashion which is easily remembered.

Here are a couple of examples I happen to find in my files:

* IVCF Canada's Focus statement:
  "Inter-Varsity Christian Fellowship is an inter-denominational mission, mobilizing Christians within Canada's educational communities to declare Jesus Christ as Saviour and Lord."

* UCCF Britain's statement:
  "UCCF works to bear witness to Jesus Christ as Saviour, Lord and God in the student world of the United Kingdom and the Republic of Ireland."

Making the Purpose Work For Us
Factors to remember:
1. Don't expect everyone has read, understood, or committed themselves to the purpose
   a. just because the purpose is written and distributed throughout the movement;
   b. just because someone has been on staff or committees for years;
   c. just because a staff team seemed to fully understand the purpose a couple of years ago.
2. Do expect that:
   a. every time a new staff member joins, or committee/board person is appointed, they will need both their own written copy of the purpose statement and a discussion about it with at least their immediate supervisor or chairman.
   b. reading and discussing the statement of purpose annually at a gathering of staff, board and committees will be helpful. Why? Because each year many opportunities and challenges face people throughout the movement which need to be held up to the searchlight of the purpose. Otherwise a worthwhile project which lies outside the purpose might erode the movement's effectiveness in carrying out its primary calling.

HINT: To get the team to take a fresh look at the purpose, open the discussion with a question like this:

> What is our primary job as a movement?
>> or,
> What should we aim to accomplish this year?
>> or,
> Within the next five years, what should we be asking God to do in/through our movement?
>> or,

Write down on a small piece of paper what you think is the main goal we need to aim for as a movement. Then collect the pages and on a large pad or chalkboard tabulate the answers. Use this as a basis for discussion

[In any interaction like this, writing people's comments on a chalkboard or large pad is a helpful way to keep the discussion moving constructively.]

2
THE ROLE
OF THE
GENERAL SECRETARY

Although our movements vary widely in size and complexity, every General Secretary is expected to give overall leadership to the entire movement. This includes leadership of all paid employees and volunteers at every level (including boards/committees, student groups, alumni, faculty). Of course, the manner in which he leads the Board of Directors to which he reports will be quite different from his leadership of paid staff. But in both cases the General Secretary is, or will become with experience, the person most completely informed about the overall ministry of the student movement.

This is not to say that he knows more about every single aspect of the movement than anyone else, nor that he is more gifted in carrying out every task that needs to be done. It simply recognizes that the General Secretary stands in a unique position in the movement to influence people who are involved at every level in the organization. Those who have given him this assignment by election or appointment have decided that he/she is the person to carry this responsibility.

One of the first responses many of us feel when given a large responsibility is "Why me?" Or, "How can I possibly do a task of this size?"

It is reassuring to study in Exodus 3 and 4 Moses' response to his calling to lead the Israelites out of Egypt.

1. Notice how specific a job description the Lord gave him at the very outset (3:7-10). How does it compare in size and complexity with your assignment as a General Secretary?

2. Immediately Moses raises questions, both about his own qualifications and about the key problems he expects to arise. Can you discern how each question Moses asks reveals a quality in his personality that shows he will make a good leader? One of the characteristics of a good leader is that he must be able to anticipate problems in order to prepare to avoid them, or at least minimize their impact.

3. Moses' response in 4:13 arouses God's anger. Do you think the Lord's anger is justified? Is there anything in your attitude to being a General Secretary that might arouse God's anger? Fortunately we have the avenue of confession and complete forgiveness (I John 1:9) with the assured help of the Holy Spirit to be with us in our tasks, working not only in our own speech, but in the lives of our colleagues.

4. If you have not yet thanked the Lord for the privilege of being a General Secretary of your movement and also thanked Him for the provision to go along with the task, take a few minutes and do so immediately. It will refresh your spirit and bond you with the Lord in a loving working relationship which will enable you to give the positive spiritual leadership which everyone in your movement needs.

I find it invigorating to thank the Lord regularly for the great privilege of serving Him among students. Then when problems arise in the work, it is easier to take that burden to God, realizing that facing problems is part of the work He has given us to do!

Take note: It was because Moses was doing God's work that he faced problems like the golden calf and the rebellious people. Had he stayed in Midian, life would have been much calmer for him.

3
BOARDS/COUNCILS

Why Do Movements Have Boards/Councils?

In order to be official members of the IFES, national movements must have a group of people from their country who formally come together and publicly establish their work. This often involves formulating a "constitution" or similar document in accordance with the legal procedures set forth by the government of the nation. Recognition by the government is often necessary to hold public meetings, open bank accounts, own property, and to employ and pay workers.

In some countries, individuals who give money to support the work are able to avoid taxation on gifts given to recognized organizations. From the standpoint of the government, the board/council is the group of people held responsible for the orderly conduct of the national student movement. Therefore it is essential that the board/council continue to function, even though the majority of the work is done by students, staff, faculty and volunteers.

In this chapter we will explore a few important aspects of both the function and relationships of the board/council in our movements. Although many of our movements face different governmental and legal requirements, the essential success factors are similar. By conversing with leaders in movements who come from your same cultural milieu you will be able to discern how others have solved problematic issues which may confront you.

What Is the Primary Role of the Board/Council?

1. To insure that the objectives spelled out in the founding document (constitution is a common term) are carried out. This customarily will include both statements of purpose and faith. IFES requires that the statement of faith be consistent with the IFES basis of faith, so if your movement is already a member of the IFES, this requirement need not concern you. However, maintaining the integrity of the purpose and statement of faith within the movement is an ongoing responsibility of the board/committee.

2. To insure that your movement meets governmental requirements for organizations such as yours. This may include such things as filing annual financial reports, withholding taxes, providing health coverage for employees, insuring that gifts are used for the ministry and not for personal gain. TV evangelists in USA have recently received nationwide news coverage for violations of the latter, and their boards are being held responsible.

Phase One: Founding

The primary task of the board/council is to see that the purpose of the movement is carried out. But must they do it themselves? Surely the task of reaching students in all of a nation's tertiary institutions is greater than the combined time and talents of its board/council?

Certainly. In every nation the vision of the founding board/council extends far beyond the potential personal resources of its members. Others must be enlisted in the task. In a small movement this may be simply board/council members plus other volunteers who are qualified. But soon even those workers become inadequate for the large task ahead and so qualified people are hired to devote their full time to the ministry. This is when the task of the board/council enters a new phase.

Phase Two: Establishing

Once people begin to serve full time with the movement, the board/council is suddenly faced with a whole new series of questions:.
* What task should this person focus on?
* To whom should he/she report?
* Who will train him/her?
* How much and how often should this person be paid?
* Who will handle financial accounts?
* Who will raise the money required?
* How should government reports be filed? By whom? When?
* How will the person's work be evaluated? How often? By whom?

All of these questions and many others will need to be answered in order to provide a wholesome climate for the ministry. Either the board/council members will need to divide up these tasks among themselves (an unlikely possibility) or decide who should handle them.

Customarily the first step is to appoint someone as "General Secretary" who can assume administrative control and in an orderly fashion handle the many details that will demand attention. Initially board/council members with professional training may assist with their skills in legal or business affairs or put the General Secretary in touch with friends who are qualified.

At this stage of development, board/council members actively participate with the General Secretary to insure that policies and procedures are established which will serve the student movement well and meet governmental requirements.

Once this initial "establishment" phase is over, the board/ Council will usually find that occasional monitoring is adequate to insure that procedures are working properly.

Phase Three: Building

Once the basic policies and procedures are in place, the movement can devote its attention to extending the ministry and increasing the base of support.

One of the characteristics of staff of young movements is their enthusiasm and singleness of purpose in helping students find Christ and establishing them in the faith. They work tirelessly to reach the thousands of students on the campuses until they near exhaustion.

At this point a wise board/council will help them realize that extended ministry may best be accomplished by increasing the base of financial and prayer support so that others may be hired to assist in the task. Board/council members may be able to assist the staff by working with them in planning ways and means of broadening the number of people who share in the ministry by prayer, volunteering for campus ministry, and/or giving financially. Church members, graduates, faculty and Christian parents of participating students all represent a potential resource which can be tapped through deliberate effort. Friends of board/council members are likewise a fine source of support.

At this stage it is very easy for a young General Secretary to feel that the board is taking over his work. The way in which the board initiates this kind of assistance is critically important. The board members must respect the integrity of the General Secretary and his staff by open discussions with them, serving as counselors, rather than as decision makers. Learning to understand one another's roles is difficult in this early stage of a movement's growth, but Christian love and mutual respect enable everyone to grow in unity and understanding. Because this differentiation is so important, the next section will give some guidelines to help both board and staff maneuver this difficult phase of development.

During the building phase, many changes and experiments are normal and even desirable. But they also call for unusual grace and patience on the part of all parties concerned. Pioneering staff will be trying out new approaches in evangelism, in training students, in assisting graduates who volunteer to help with the student ministry. Some of these experiments may fail. Others may arouse the ire of church leaders who feel that a certain approach is inappropriate. Both the staff members and board members in this phase will need to exercise some, if not all, of the following:

patience	listening
love	asking questions
prayer	Biblical study
openness	sharing hopes, fears.

Open communication is very important in every phase of Christian work, but particularly in this developmental stage when new experiences are commonplace. The staff must not withhold information about failed experiments from board/council and the board/council must be very open in its dialogue with staff as to hopes, fears, questions, etc. Open dialogue followed by prayer together as board and staff members will pave the way for good working relationships in the future and help maintain unity despite the many new experiences and some surprises which emerge from ministry experiments.

Interaction with the IFES regional or associate General Secretary for your part of the world can be invaluable in broadening the perspective of people in both board/council and staff. His/her experience in other nations will add a depth of understanding which will often clarify ambiguous or controversial interpretations of developments in the movement.

If it hasn't been done earlier, it is in this stage that job descriptions need to be formulated for board/council members. By now this project could be undertaken by board/council members and staff working together. This will enable both groups to understand one another better and clarify areas which overlap. And it may also reveal gaps which need to be filled. This will also be a good time for board/council members to update their understanding of staff job descriptions.

Guidelines Defining Board/Council and Staff Roles

Although there is no passage of Scripture which clearly defines the various roles that should be played by board/council members and staff people, experience and common sense lead us to several basic principles.

1. The board/council is ultimately responsible for the fulfillment of the purposes outlined in the constituting documents.

2. The board/council delegates to the staff team the task of carrying out the purpose in the educational institutions.

3. The board/council members have authority over staff people only when they are meeting together as a board. This avoids the problem of staff having multiple "bosses" who may issue conflicting instructions. An exception to this is when a board/council member is also a staff person. In that case the direct leadership of the board/council member is confined to his own bailiwick when he is not in a board meeting.

4. The board/council gives overall leadership to the movement, and establishes procedures which enable the staff people to carry out the work. The tools of the board/council are reports from staff, long-range and annual plans presented by staff to board/council, budgets, and interaction with staff people at board/council meetings. The first-hand observation of ministry in the board members' own geo-

graphic areas will inform them to some extent of what is happening at the grass roots. But apart from informal interaction with staff, no formal instructions can be given by board/council members at that level. If a board/council member wishes to recommend action, it must be done through the board/council meeting, or perhaps in conversation with the General Secretary.

5. The General Secretary is customarily the person whom the board/council holds responsible for the work and so it is important that they communicate with each other openly and regularly.

6. As the movement grows, the board/council should establish procedures to enable it to interact regularly with representative staff from various levels of the organization. It should also insure that procedures are established to handle grievances.

7. The General Secretary should set up necessary mechanisms to facilitate communication between board/council and staff. Board/council decisions need to be shared with staff, and staff opinion shared with board/council so that board/council members can make informed decisions.

8. At all times the aim of people in every level of the organization should be to develop ONE TEAM, so that whether a person serves on staff or on the board/council, he considers the national movement his family. Neither should develop a life of its own without the other. Both are vital to the well-being of the movement. Both serve our Lord. Both serve students.

A Typical Life-Cycle of Board/Council and Staff Relationships

When a movement is just beginning, the board/council will know much more about the purpose and approach of the ministry than anyone else.

When a movement is just beginning, the board/council will know much more about the purpose and approach of the ministry than anyone else.

After the General Secretary and staff have served for a year or more, they will inevitably understand many aspects of the student work better than most, if not all, board/council members. Furthermore, after several years the founding members of the movement will probably have been replaced or supplemented by others, so that the vision of the original board/council members will need to be imparted to these new participants. Often this can best be done by the staff, rather than fellow board/council members. In light of these factors, the following diagram not only describes the changing role of the board/council with staff, but it also depicts a desirable trend in a national movement.

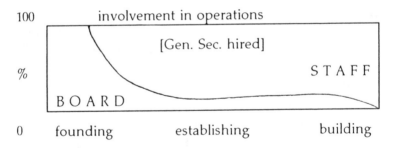

Think About These Scriptures
. . . everything should be done in a fitting and orderly way. (1 Cor 14:40)

. . . speaking the truth in love, we will in all things grow up into him who is the Head, that is Christ. From him the whole body, joined and held together by every supporting ligament, grows and builds itself up in love, as each part does its work. (Eph. 4:15,16)

There are different kinds of gifts, but the same Spirit. There are different kinds of service, but the same Lord. There are different kinds of working, but the same God works all of them in all men. (1 Cor. 12:4-6)

Now to each one the manifestation of the Spirit is given for the common good. (1 Cor. 12:7)

You know that the rulers of the Gentiles lord it over them, and their high officials exercise authority over them. Not so with you. Instead, whoever wants to become great among you must be your servant, and whoever wants to be first must be your slave just as the Son of Man did not come to be served, but to serve, and to give his life as a ransom for many. (Matt. 20:25-28)

Everyone must submit himself to the governing authorities, for there is no authority except that which God has established. The authorities that exist have been established by God. (Romans 13:1)

For further study:
 John White, *Excellence in Leadership*, Downers Grove, IL, InterVarsity Press, 1986.
 Chua Wee Hian, *Learning to Lead*, Downers Grove, IL, Inter Varsity Press, 1987.
 John W. Alexander, *Managing Our Work*, Downers Grove, IL, InterVarsity Press, 1972.

4
JOB DESCRIPTIONS-
BOARD/COUNCIL

People are often surprised when one suggests that board/council members deserve a job description. Job descriptions for employees? Yes, by all means. But for council members? Why, they're volunteering their time so one surely can't expect them to agree to a specific job description. That's expecting too much of working people who already lead a busy life and must do volunteer work during their leisure hours.

On the contrary, consider these positive reasons for clearly defining the job of a board/council member:

1. In recruitment: When a person is invited to join the board/council, a clear job description a) gives board and staff people a consistent way of describing the task to be done; and b) gives invitees a written expression of what is expected of them which they can take home, show to their spouse, and pray about. It may also give them a sense that your movement takes board/council membership seriously.

2. In orientation: From the very first meeting of the board/council, the new member has an idea of his role in the organization, and should not be surprised by what others expect of him. This should free him to take a more active role earlier in his tenure.

3. In board/council meetings: The written job description gives members the freedom to initiate queries regarding matters that their job description articulates. It also gives them a basis to assist the chairman in keeping the focus of the board/council on its main target; for example, to help

the board/council make policy decisions, rather than operational ones.

4. In discipline: Members who are not doing their part can be warned of specific failures, based on their mutually agreed job definition.

How Do We Go About Composing a Job Description for Board/Council Members?

As we mentioned in the previous chapter on boards, a mature movement board/council and staff can work together in developing the job descriptions for council members. A General Secretary who believes it would be wise to formalize job descriptions for board/council can properly discuss the idea in private with the chairman of the board/council. Or the board/council chairman may initiate dialogue with both the General Secretary and some of his council colleagues.

Some of the questions to be answered will include the following:

1. What are the primary functions of our board/council? Are these clearly stated in our official documents?

2. In what ways will formal job descriptions help us accomplish our purpose? (Especially note ambiguities, conflicts or inaction that may result from unclear guidelines.)

3. What are our present a) written and b) unwritten expectations of a board/council member?

4. Are we satisfied with the way our board/council is functioning now? If not, what changes are needed? How could any of these changes be effected by entries in a job description for board/council members?

Drafting a Job Description can best be done by a small group appointed by the chairman of the board/council. When good relationships exist between board and staff, it will be natural for the chairman to include at least one staff person on such a small committee. The wise chairman will know the value of having staff involved, since they see the inner workings of the movement most intimately.

Once this group has composed a first draft, it should then be reviewed by the chairman and General Secretary. If they are satisfied, it may then be presented to the entire board for their input before adoption.

Don't be surprised if there is vigorous discussion over various aspects of the proposal. This kind of interaction will be a tonic to members' understanding of the role of the board/council.

What If There is Resistance to the Term "Job Description"?

If some members feel that such terminology should be reserved for staff people, choose a term more acceptable. Possibilities include

"Position Description",

"Expectations of council members",

"Responsibilities of council members."

What Categories Should Be Included in Such a Position Description?

1. SPIRITUAL/MORAL - Personal commitment to Christ, readiness to sign the Basis of Faith of the movement, and living a Christ-like life.

2. COMMITMENT TO PURPOSE - Wholehearted agreement with the movement's statement of purpose and commitment to give time, talent and money in helping the movement fulfill its purpose.

3. AGREEMENT WITH STYLE OF MINISTRY - Among Christian churches and movements there are wide varieties of style in ministry. Board/council members should not come aboard with the idea of making radical changes in a

style of ministry which your movement has found effective over the years. Board/council members should appreciate the positive features of the ministry styles, so their influence will not be contentious, but constructive.

4. PARTICIPATION AT LOCAL LEVEL - A board/council member will be able to understand and contribute much more if he/she is involved in ministry in a local area, either on campus or in an ancillary ministry such as a prayer group or sponsoring committee.

5. ATTENDANCE - Regular board/council attendance and committee participation are appropriate expectations.

How About Some Examples?

CANADA - In the Canadian IVCF, a large group of over 400 friends scattered across Canada make up what is called the Corporation. A small group of these people constitute the Board, who take an active role in overseeing the work of IVCF. Notice how 1) Corporation and Board responsibilities interleave in the descriptions which follow, and 2) the way in which a written statement of what a board does while in session clarifies the members' responsibilities.

Responsibilities of a Corporation Member

An IVCF Corporation member is expected:

a. to be one in whose life the fruits of the Holy Spirit are evident.

b. to be a member of a local church or assembly and to participate regularly in Christian fellowship.

c. to attend the meetings of the Corporation.

d. to give financially in proportion to one's ability, demonstrating unusually strong interest in IVCF.

e. to sign each year the Statement of Agreement.

f. to participate in an area committee.

g. to encourage staff members in their work.

h. to be involved in some way with the life of an IVCF ministry.

i. to pray regularly for Inter-Varsity by using the various "Intercessors."

j. to inform friends and others about the ministry of IVCF.

Responsibilities of a Board Member

The Board Member of IVCF:

a. Fulfills with distinction the responsibilities of an IVCF corporation member.

b. Participates jointly with other members in carrying out the responsibilities listed for the Board as a corporate whole.

c. Accepts appointment to board commissions.

d. Attends board meetings and meetings of assigned board commissions.

e. Performs the study and homework prerequisite for board meetings and commission meetings.

f. Acquires a broad knowledge of IVCF.

g. Provides advice and counsel to Management, but refrains from involvement in management.

h. Identifies situations in which he/she has special competence or contacts and makes these known to the Board and the General Director.

Responsibility of the Board Chairman

The Board Chairman of IVCF:

a. reviews with the General Director his recommended policies, plans, budgets and personnel appointments and recommends them to the Board.

b. reviews with the General Director the progress and problems of Management, and sees that Management carries out the expressed wishes of the Board.

c. sees that the Board and Corporation Members are adequately informed on affairs of IVCF.

d. calls meetings of the Board and of the Corporation, approves the agenda and presides at the meetings.

e. guides the Board in fulfilling responsibilities.

f. draws from Trustees optimum participation and contribution.

g. directs the Board toward board matters and away from the management matters.

h. appoints board committees and their chairmen and assures effective functioning of these commissions.

i. carries out duties specified in the By-laws.

Responsibilities of the Board in Session
The Board of Directors of the Canadian IVCF:

a. Sets the course of IVCF as a Movement: Is responsible for the formulation of major policy and long-range plans.

b. Reserves selected powers of decision making.

c. Delegates all other powers.

d. Elects the Chief Executive Officer.

e. Approves appointment of staff reporting directly to the chief executive officer.

f. Provides advice, counsel and assistance to Management.

g. Approves the budget.

h. Approves major capital expenditures.

i. Reviews the progress of the Movement and takes appropriate action.

j. Creates adequate machinery for fulfilling Board responsibilities, including perpetuation of a healthy Board.

k. Submits to the Corporation those proposals requiring Corporation approval.

l. Identifies the Board's needs for information from Management.

Student Members

When a board/council includes student representatives,
their position description should include at least these three
additional entries:

1. In consultation with staff, a) to present to fellow chapter
leaders the relevant issues under consideration by board/
council, b) to listen to the various responses of these
students so they can be accurately communicated to board/
council as the opportunity arises.

2. To share in Board/Council sessions the perspective of the
current academic scene, and in particular to represent the
outlook of the student members of the national movement;

3. To communicate to the students in the movement, in
consultation with the General Secretary and staff, the
decisions of the board/council which are relevant to student
participants.

Staff Members

Although from time to time almost every movement will
find it wise to invite various staff department heads or
specialists to advise the board/council in session, some
movements choose to add several staff members to the
board/council.

When staff members, in addition to the General Secretary,
are full members of board/council, they will tend to focus
their attention in the area of their prime responsibility. Fair
enough. But they also possess insights and general wisdom
which will enrich the understanding of the entire board/
council. Therefore it will be wise to include in their job
descriptions a specific entry which affirms that they are
responsible to participate as full members.

What Does the Ideal Board/Council Member Do in Council Meetings?

LISTENS - ASKS - LEARNS

EVALUATES - PROBES - COMPARES - EXTRAPOLATES (considers what this decision will mean in years ahead)

COUNTS THE COST - in staff effort, money

VISUALIZES - what this decision will mean to campus, community and church

CONNECTS - resources within his network which may meet needs which are identified during council discussions

SPEAKS - about aspects that he believes are important or may have been overlooked or inadequately presented

COMMENDS - ENCOURAGES - AFFIRMS both staff and board colleagues whose contributions have been salutary

PRAYS - silently and/or publicly as various matters are presented

DECIDES/VOTES - using best judgment without partiality

5
PLANNING

Whether we give it a name or not, all of us involved in ministry make plans. We plan appointments with students, or make an itinerary for a trip. We plan the theme of a conference or talk. We have a call from a group asking for assistance, and so we plan how to meet that need. Every person on a staff team will recognize these activities as a part of normal staff ministry.

However, the General Secretary of a movement needs to devote extra attention to planning. Why so?

1. MOST LEADERS DO SO. It is recognized in management circles that senior leaders spend proportionately more time in planning than those working for them. This means that in our movements, the General Secretary will probably need to spend more time in planning than other members of the team.

2. THE WORK DEMANDS IT. The way in which the vision or overall purpose of the movement is carried out needs to be defined by the leadership. And the larger the number of people involved, the more complex the plan. If every individual is to understand his part in fulfilling the vision, he must be made aware of what colleagues around him are doing and how his own assignment can be harmonized with theirs. Then as he drafts a plan for his own work, his understanding of the overall ministry will avoid major revamping later. [Note how the conductor of an orchestra spends all of his time synchronizing the music of all the players. Although he may be able to play several instruments well, when he conducts a large orchestra, he only conducts. If the ensemble is small, he may also be able to

play an instrument in concert. The same general rule
applies to a General Secretary.]

3. IT ENHANCES PARTICIPATION. Planning enables
others in the organization to contribute to the direction the
organization is going, if the leader provides a means of
participation. Without planning, most members of a team
will be forced to do only what they are told, without
understanding the overall strategy. Participation enables
them to pray and work with a large group of people in
attaining the common objective. [If the movement is
working toward the establishment of new groups in 20
colleges, and if the leaders share this vision, the entire team
can pray and work out specific plans for reaching their
share of the colleges. And the board/committee members
can participate in prayer and often assist in their local
areas.]

4. IT INCREASES THE MINISTRY. Planning also protects
a General Secretary from doing ministry which others can
carry out. When an advance plan is developed, other
members of the team can be enlisted to perform tasks that
would otherwise be known only to the leader. By letting
others participate, more work will almost always be
accomplished, AND the overworked General Secretary will
be spared burnout.

The Lord has plans also:

> For I know the plans I have for you, says the Lord,
> plans for welfare and not for evil, to give you a
> future and a hope. (Jeremiah 29:11)

> . . . for he has made known to us in all wisdom and
> insight the mystery of his will, according to his
> purpose which he set forth in Christ as a plan for the

fullness of time, to unite all things in him, things in heaven and things on earth. (Ephesians 1:9,10)

Planning is the process by which we determine how we intend to carry out our vision or objective. The vision must always come first, so that the plan of action has a focus.

But at the same time, our plans are not sacred nor infallible. Plans are our servants to assist us in carrying out the vision. They are subject to review and change, since we work in a world where change is commonplace. Who could have accurately planned for the multiple changes which accompany the international monetary crisis?

Experience is an excellent teacher, so I am summarizing here an interview with Peter Northrup, a member of the IFES leadership team. Peter was engaged in student ministry with IVCF-USA for over 30 years and intimately involved in every level of planning in a national movement. We are grateful to have his insights.

Q> Is planning Biblical? I have talked with people who say that if we are led by God's Spirit, we needn't bother to plan . . . just do what He says at the moment.

A> The Bible helps us in answering that, as in Exodus 3 and 4 we read how God had a plan and as a result he:
  chose a man,
  told him where to go, and
  what to do if the Egyptians didn't respond.
But he also continued with them in the pillar of fire and cloud.

Q> Both/and?

A> Yes, exactly. Always planning and always action in process by the Holy Spirit. The Holy Spirit is always taking your plans and massaging (interacting with) them.

Q> How do your plans become God's, or vice versa?

A> In Moses' case the plan was revealed to him because the plan was so foreign to anything Moses would have experienced. And God may lead us, too, into those situations. But usually the Holy Spirit interacts as the leader and his team plan together.

Q> What should a Spirit-led team do?

A> First, decide what their objectives are. Identify or reaffirm their purpose statement. As they prayerfully depend on the Holy Spirit, they will experience His help in determining what they are planning for.

Q> Can you identify the parameters of this planning process?

A> At the student group level plans will include:

Individual plans for personal life and ministry.

Plans for what to do as a group.

Plans for how to train/influence others.

Another approach is to:

1. Spot objectives.
2. Ask, "What action must we take to get to the objective?"
3. Discover the resources we have to muster to bring it about.

To illustrate: In meeting an evangelism objective, ask: How is evangelism going? A key indicator will be students talking with their friends about the Lord Jesus, not simply whether the group has had evangelism training. Remember that one may hold training sessions in evangelism without anyone becoming a Christian. In this case another approach is to pray that one or more in the group be given a gift of evangelism.

Another illustration: Point 3, "discovering resources," can be handled by asking "What resources do we already have?" and also "What resources do we need to pray and work for to bring about the desired result?" This way we first focus on what God has already given us.

Q> Please elaborate on the kinds of resources.

A> Almost always our prime resource is people who are gifted by the Holy Spirit to do the job. The temple had its

Ahimelech. If you're Moses in the wilderness, you need judges of 1000's, 100's, 50's, and tens.

Q> Is it possible to overplan? What are the dangers in planning?

A> The biggest danger is expectations which are too high. In your enthusiasm to work for the Lord you outstrip His objectives. Because your objectives have been so grandiose, the plan collapses before it gets anywhere near completion, with the result that everyone becomes discouraged and wonders why the Holy Spirit isn't doing anything. And some will abandon trying at all.

The other extreme is to be so fearful (or self-centered or something) that the vision is limited to objectives which are solely attainable through human strength. The key is in setting realistic objectives.

Q> Other dangers?

A> Not keeping an eye on the purpose. I remember visiting the Inter-Varsity chapter at Kutztown where the IV group had become only a political action group. So I asked them for a copy of the constitution and statement of purpose. In focusing on "Why are we here?" the conflict became clear. And in that case they redirected their action into evangelism and began reaching out.

Q> Planning in our student movement is new to us. What is available to help us plan?

A> Some student movements have planning materials to assist staff teams in planning. Others have handbooks for student groups to assist them. Check with the older student movements in your part of the world for examples of what they have found helpful.

Q> What are the major components of a balanced student ministry?

A> Evaluate your objectives to make sure they're not "hobby horses", but develop all aspects of the purpose. As a matter of fact, I think God takes us down one heavy avenue . . . e.g. witness, prayer, Bible study, some Christian disciplines. There is an ebb and flow to the whole process, an ORGANIC development.

Incidentally, when you're planning, expect some of these things to happen:
- violent, vigorous disagreement in deciding emphasis
- distraction
- pet projects.

Q> What are some ways out of pitfalls?
A> ■ A great deal of prayer,
- a sense of community or team work,
- a recognition of a call to the work,
- a variety of gifts (team),
- the voice of experience (advice from mature people),
- listening ear to complications being encountered.

In the additional pitfall of a failure to follow a healthy management cycle (planning, organizing, implementing, evaluating), it is helpful to think practically about who, what, when, where, why and how to proceed. These questions assist us in analyzing our work in concrete sequential steps. We also need the patience to keep them in the proper order, e.g. not spending money until it is received, etc.

Q> Have you ideas for a sample team planning agenda?
A> 1. Choose a proper location.
2. Reaffirmation of purpose by the entire group. Break it down into smaller segments, e.g. evangelism, discipleship, missions., and break evangelism into possible kinds of evangelism you might have. A small group purpose might be to have two Bible discussions with non-Christians, and individuals talking with their friends. If yours is a large group, you might aim to proclaim the Gospel in a large event and/or establish an evangelistic booktable.
3. Analysis of where we are in light of this purpose.

4. Identify where God wants us, when. (sorting priorities, time frame)

5. Make an action plan. State how to get to each objective.

For example, if in evangelism we have identified where we are, (many willing to speak to friends) we may discern that God wants us to add group discussion to help break through some of the barriers. Therefore, we proceed to:

a. Identify who should be discussion leader.

b. Locate or prepare useful discussion resource material (if available).

c. Plan prayer support team to back up those in the group.

d. Answer logistical questions related to when, where, etc. It is customary that the closer to the event, the more specific and detailed the plan. Usually at the group executive level, the planning period is the academic term.

e. Then realistically uncover resources you have, e.g. people to do things or money to buy Bibles for people in small groups.

6. Communicate the plan. "Processing it through the group" is another way of expressing this important step.

a. The purpose: reminder of what God has called us to do.

b. The plan: helping other members of the group understand the plan and commit themselves to doing the work.

Communicating the plan takes more than a written plan or an announcement to the group. Walk people through it. Commit valuable time to bring the group along with you:

Share individually with key members.

Explain at a large group meeting the process you went through in formulating the plan.

Get reaction, feedback and corrections to the plan.

is it too grandiose?

insufficiently visionary?

timing wrong?
Then invite members to help identify resources and to commit themselves.

Note: 2nd time around, it'll be easier. Don't hesitate to listen to the Holy Spirit and one another; and be prepared to adjust in midstream.

Some Final Thoughts
National plans - 2+ years ahead
Regional plans - 1 year ahead
Local plans - 2 semesters ahead
Prayer is vital at every stage.

"Without me, you can do nothing." (John 15:5)

Some Thoughts on Long-Range Planning
Although the Lord has an eternal plan, humans face so many factors over which they have no control that a firm, unchangeable long-range plan is futile.

Some management theories advocate long-range planning for 5 to 10 years, although more recently some experts have advised a 3-year plan as more realistic.

In a student movement, some aspects of ministry can be included in a long-range vision for the ministry. Appointment of personnel for 3 or 5 years, or a target of having chapters composed of 10% of the student body, or increasing the staff team by one person each year for the next five years may all be attainable objectives.

But the specific plans as to who will do what 3 to 5 years hence may be subject to so many uncontrollable factors that careful planning will be a waste of time. Nevertheless, envisioning these possibilities will fuel prayer and stimulate immediate strategies which will ultimately make the vision a reality.

As a general rule, the most useful plan looks one-year ahead. And if a staff team every 3 months reviews the work of the previous quarter and looks at its plan one year hence, it will find the planning much less burdensome. Why? Because most of our ministry falls into an annual pattern, and as we review the work of the previous quarter and lay final plans for the quarter ahead, we will find it easy to conceive what we may want to improve next year. And often what we aspire to do in the next 3 months may need to be pared back and delayed until the following year. [If geography and money prohibit quarterly meetings, written reports can cover these topics quarterly.]

The following chart expresses this:
　　Staff meeting in Dec 87:
　　Review work of Oct-Dec 87
　　Plan details of Jan-Mar 88 & general plan of Oct-Dec 88
　　　　(same quarter next year)
In addition, once per year the team should review an entire year and then also make its full-year annual plan.

6
DECISIONS

Whether we like it or not, leadership involves making decisions. The General Secretary of a movement is expected to
    establish goals,
        determine priorities,
            hire workers,
                assign duties,
                    evaluate performance,
                        and insure that biblical standards are
                        maintained throughout the movement.

Every one of these functions involves a series of decisions: affirming one course of action while declining perhaps hundreds of alternatives.

The same is true of the board/council of a movement. Any well-run board/council will maintain a minute book in which each of its decisions is recorded. Although discussions over a period of months may precede a decision, the minute book succinctly records the final decision for posterity. What does this indicate? That the board/council considers its decisions important, and intends that they be implemented.

We as Christians have an exceptional resource in decision-making: THE INDWELLING HOLY SPIRIT. To enlarge our understanding of the Holy Spirit's role in decision-making, it is worthwhile studying how Jesus and the early apostles made their decisions. We learn, for example, that the practice of fasting and prayer was commonly associated with strategic decision-making. The entire church was involved in many aspects of discerning the course of action to take, and even our Lord asked Peter, James and John to watch with him in Gethsemane as he battled through his impending death.

In this context we are reminded that our decisions also involve struggles between our personal preferences and the will of God. May we have the grace to say, as Jesus did, "Nevertheless, not my will, but thine be done."

Passages such as Acts 13:1-3 succinctly illustrate the process of making a decision. And the letter from the church in Jerusalem to the believers in Antioch reflects their awareness of the activity of the Holy Spirit when they write, "It seemed good to the Holy Spirit and to us . . ." (Acts 15:28). A board/council and staff leadership team, meeting together, could benefit greatly by studying a few of these key passages.

Wise Decisions Can Be Made When . . . .
1. There is a CLEAR STATEMENT of PURPOSE. Unless we know in what direction we are heading, we can't tell whether we're on the right track.
2. The INFORMATION BASE is true to reality. As we've noted before, "a person's judgment is only as good as his information."
3. The APPROPRIATE PEOPLE are making the decision. If an issue to be decided lies outside the decision-maker's sphere of control, even a wise decision can suddenly cause a host of problems.
4. REASONABLE ALTERNATIVES have been openly considered. It is often tempting to present a strong, water-tight case for something you deeply desire, in an effort to prevent other people involved from seriously considering viable alternatives. This weakens the information/judgment base.

5. THE TIMING IS RIGHT. A correct decision made at the wrong time (too late, for example) can weaken or invalidate the decision.

Determining Who Should Make a Decision

Both board/council and General Secretary regularly take actions that determine where decisions are made. A board/council customarily makes decisions that cover broad areas, leaving to the administrative staff the detailed choices that necessarily follow.

Once a General Secretary is well acquainted with the work, he will take the initiative in presenting to the board the decisions that must be made. He will need to decide which matters are most urgently needing attention, and then determine whether that issue needs to be brought forward for board action.

How Does the General Secretary Learn Which Issues Require Board/Council Action?

1. FROM LEGAL REQUIREMENTS

a. Changes in the Constitution, By-laws, and other legal documents require action by the board/council.

b. The board/council bears overall responsibility for the financial health of the organization. Customarily the board exercises its control through approval of the annual budget of income and expenses.

c. Since board/council members are volunteers, they must hire staff to carry out the management and work of the movement.

Customarily they hire a General Secretary, who may recommend for appointment other staff. In practice, as a movement grows larger, its board/council may authorize the General Secretary to handle the appointment of all except the senior staff who report directly to the General Secretary.

d. Real estate transactions involving title-deeds and mortgage documents customarily require an officially-minuted vote of approval by the board/council.

2. FROM THE BOARD/COUNCIL CHAIRMAN

Ideally, the chairman of the board/council and General Secretary meet together between board/council meetings to talk over the work of the movement. They learn from one another:

a. The CHAIRMAN learns from the General Secretary about the work of the movement and the issues facing the staff. A good chairman will ask probing questions to come to as complete an understanding as possible. This may mean, at times, that various staff people may be invited to join the discussion between board/council meetings, as well as during the meetings themselves. This should not threaten the General Secretary, but give him a broader hearing. Furthermore, it will help the board/council people to come to a better understanding of the issues facing the staff.

b. The General Secretary learns from the chairman

- his perspective on whether the issue at hand requires board action,
- the outlook of the board/council members,
- the kinds of questions they are likely to raise in reviewing the issues,
- and the extent to which written documentation is desired.

While working together, the chairman of the board/council will help the General Secretary learn which issues require a decision by the board/council and which ones can be decided by staff.

3. FROM THE BOARD/COUNCIL MINUTES

By browsing through minutes of the board/council, the General Secretary will be able to observe the kinds of issues which have been considered by the board. But this is not necessarily an ideal means of determining what should be done now. Why? Because as a movement matures, the kinds of issues dealt with by the board/council change.

a. When a movement is small and board/council members are heavily involved in student ministry alongside staff, council meetings naturally deal with meeting plans and coordination of the work at a level which is later covered by staff. (See ADMINISTRY #4, "Boards/Councils")

b. Sometimes a board/council retains control to an unhealthy extent, thus depriving staff of the authority which should rightly be theirs. When a General Secretary finds himself in this situation, he should prayerfully seek to bring about a change, via open dialogue with the chairman. If the chairman himself is unable to understand this, prayer, patience and the counsel of your IFES regional secretary will help effect change in a godly way.

c. If the previous General Secretary worked with his board/council in formulating policies outlining proper ways of handling affairs of the movement, your task will be much easier.

What Is a Policy?

I've always found it helpful to follow the advice of someone who said to me many years ago, "If you find you are having to answer the same question more than once or twice, you should begin to think about formulating a policy." In these terms a policy is a formal statement of how anyone in the organization should handle certain situations. Policies can deal with a wide range of situations in the fields of personnel, finance, ministry guidelines, administrative structures, and tangibles such as real estate and equipment purchases.

Although staff may groan (as I have been known to do myself) when a new, thick policy manual is distributed, clear policies are far better than the whimsical, unpredictable pattern that emerges when a group of people try to function together without some basic agreements. Imagine a soccer game without basic rules. The game would hardly begin before irate players would walk off the field.

Beginning a national movement is a little like starting a game without a rule book. Yes, we have the Bible as our basic book. But biblical principles need to be applied with definite statements about salary levels, reporting policies, handling expenses, kinds of staff to recruit, etc. Both board/council and staff of an emerging student movement are well advised to look over the shoulders (and minute and policy books) of sister movements to learn what kinds of decisions lie ahead of them.

Ultimately, the board/council and General Secretary will be spared many individual decisions if they make generic decisions (policies) covering situations that are likely to recur throughout the movement.

Decision Check-List
Here are some questions to ask during the decision-making process:
1. Is this the right person or group to make this decision?
2. Could we make a more basic decision than this that would solve similar issues in the future? (become a policy)
3. Have we looked at the implications of this decision for each aspect of our work?
4. Have we the resources to enable this decision to be implemented? (people, time, money, etc.)
5. Will this decision be fair to all parties involved?

6. Does this decision strengthen the fulfillment of our purpose?
7. Have we openly considered alternative approaches? (Has anyone championed other solutions to sharpen our thinking, or have they all been kept under cover?)
8. Do we know of any forthcoming event that might affect the validity of this decision, positively or negatively?
9. Have we listened to various levels of staff who are or should be concerned about this matter?
10. Does this decision fully coincide with Biblical principles?
11. Who will need to do what to carry out this decision?
12. How and when will we monitor
   a. whether this decision is being carried out?
   b. how beneficial it is?

A good decision is one which benefits the movement by:
   enhancing its ability to fulfill its purpose; and
   enabling its participants at both board/council and staff levels to work harmoniously together.

If your movement has not yet prepared a policy manual, prayerfully seek someone who has an orderly mind and some administrative experience to begin gathering and formulating statements that will become your policy manual. A capable secretary can do an effective job of searching previous board/council minutes to tabulate all previous actions which might become a formalized policy.

In addition, many movements will have memoranda from the General Secretary or national movement office that should be considered for inclusion. There may even be a large body of unspoken policy which needs to be written. As you work through the minutes, other entries will come to mind that need articulation.

This preliminary listing may then be organized by topic and reviewed for its coherence (some decisions may conflict with one another) and relevance.

When this task is completed, the members of staff and board should be involved in reviewing it, perhaps in a joint committee of selected board/council and staff. The resulting document could then become the policy manual of the organization.

Should the board/council approve this policy manual? Not necessarily. It may be kept as an administrative document which can thus be more easily adapted to suit the changing demands of the work. Only those policies which might conflict with previous board action would need to be reviewed and changed by a formal minute of the board/council.

Delegating Decision-Making

Delegation is a common word to express the action of a General Secretary when he asks someone else to make decisions.

A wise leader will expect members of his team to make many decisions, even as a wise board/council will expect the General Secretary and his team to carry the brunt of day-to-day decision-making in the movement.

A problem occurs when people don't trust those to whom they are delegating decision-making. Without confidence in one's co-workers, one either makes all decisions himself, or lives with fear and trepidation. Thus effective delegation of decision-making requires a) hiring and training the right people to work on the team, and b) insuring that potential board/council members are properly screened.

Of course any person who joins the staff or board/council will need both orientation and some experience before his decisions are reliable. Those in charge of each level in the movement need to be sensitive to these new people, patiently providing them with background information and responding readily to their questions.

A new worker among students will need much more help in decision-making than someone of experience. Leaders who are sensitive will stay in prayerful dialogue with each individual, giving them increasing decision-making authority as their experience and understanding increase.

Occasionally one will encounter staff or board/council people who rush brashly ahead and make decisions which someone else is authorized to make. By loving rebuke and careful explication of why the decision lies in someone else's bailiwick, the individual may be helped to act more appropriately in the future.

7
COMMUNICATION

If one had to select key factors that are essential to the success of a student movement, good communication would surely be one of them.

Without effective communication, a host of difficulties ensue:

    misunderstandings,
    missed appointments,
    conflicting aims,
    duplication of effort,
    lack of community spirit,
    and dozens of other trends that erode morale and
      fracture a fellowship.

Although non-verbal communication commands much attention today, in this chapter we will focus on verbal communication, since it is central to leadership.

In the normal course of his work, the General Secretary communicates with the Lord, his superiors, his colleagues on the staff, students, faculty, business contacts, pastors, donors, graduates, and a host of others. He uses face-to-face dialogue, telephone, letters, printed materials, and perhaps audio and video tapes. He meets people individually, speaks to groups of people in various settings, and may engage in discussion at committee and team level. All of these form the communication network which enables him to do his job.

TWO-WAY COMMUNICATION.   Listening should occupy at least half of the time any leader spends in contact with people, unless he is in a formal speaking situation.

And it is not surprising that the work of the team together is stronger and wiser than that of the General Secretary alone.

Communicating with the Board/Council

One of the most challenging aspects of leadership in a movement is providing adequate communication between the board/council and staff.

Although it is customary for the board/council to delegate to the staff the day-to-day student work, the ultimate responsibility for fulfilling the purpose lies with the board. But how will they know if the purpose is being fulfilled without adequate information? And how does the General Secretary determine what is adequate information?

A small Christian organization with which I am acquainted had a custom of sending to each board member a copy of each staff person's report. This saved the General Secretary a lot of work and gave full information to every board member. But it became cumbersome as the size of the staff grew to a dozen, and the end result was that the reports were not read and communication was thwarted. Furthermore, the board members did not receive the evaluation of the General Secretary, nor the response of the General Secretary to the staff. What appeared to be full information was, in reality, only partial.

What, then, are the best ways of handling communication between the staff and the board?

Many possibilities exist, but perhaps the essential features should include the following:

1. An honest description of what is happening in the movement:
   * in the schools
   * among graduates
   * among the staff

   * in the community (church, campus)
   * in the office and life of the General Secretary.

Comparative information from the previous year and how well goals and plans have been reached are helpful perspectives.

2. A description of problems which are faced in any/each of the above categories.

3. A status report on income and expenditure, as compared with the same period a year ago.

4. A view ahead--plans, expectations.

5. An annotated listing of decisions by the board which the General Secretary believes are needed. Full information should be available about significant aspects of any such decision, but it is usually helpful to have a summary of salient points on a cover sheet.

If the board/council is meeting monthly some of the above items may be handled quarterly or annually. But if so, the cycle should be agreed in advance.

In fact, regardless of board frequency, it is helpful to work out an annual cycle of agenda items so that the staff have time to prepare carefully. A planned agenda will also avoid careless omissions.

Communication between board/council and the staff is sometimes handled exclusively by the General Secretary. Why? Positively, it insures that the General Secretary is kept fully informed and controls information flow to the staff. Negatively, it means that the board may get a very limited picture of what is happening in the movement. This is particularly true if the General Secretary wishes to conceal problems or if complex issues are being considered which lie outside the expertise of the General Secretary.

Perhaps the healthiest approach is to have representatives from the staff attend board meetings with freedom to participate. If the General Secretary is leading properly, this should not be a threat, but should enhance the understanding and commitment of members of his team.

Remember that a council's JUDGMENT is only as good as its INFORMATION. And it is also good to note that REFLECTION ENHANCES WISDOM. Surprising a board by calling for an unexpected decision is rarely wise. Advance warning by letter, phone, or face-to-face visit is far better. The extra time, effort and expense involved are well worth the increased wisdom which results.

Communicating with Staff

When a movement is small, communication takes place in face-to-face encounters. Members get to know one another in various settings and spontaneously develop relationships which provide the necessary communication. While meeting together to plan conferences, to carry out workshops or to engage in ministry to students, the staff learn to know the General Secretary, and he comes to know them. Such intimate working conditions rarely require much paperwork or formal procedures. A kind of family spirit prevails and members spontaneously care for one another. However, as a movement grows the General Secretary must implement new methods of communicating the movement's vision. He must also devise ways and means whereby he listens to the staff and learns what is actually happening in their lives and in the student work.

What are some of the ways in which this has been accomplished most effectively?

Communications from the General Secretary

* A periodic newsletter either from the General Secretary himself or from someone in the national office. The frequency should be not less than monthly; many movements find a weekly cycle desirable. It is wise for the

General Secretary himself to have a column in the newsletter at least monthly, sharing his vision, some experiences, and selecting news from various workers. He may also wish to share insights from Scripture which have been meaningful to him. The tone should customarily be pastoral, including appropriate exhortation and teaching.

* Prompt and courteous response to all reports and letters that come to him from staff. Staff deserve high priority in correspondence. If the General Secretary is traveling for an extended period, acknowledgement of receipt should be sent by someone in the office, giving an indication of when a reply may be expected. [If responding to reports becomes burdensome, it may be wise for the leaders to delegate work to associates who will respond to reports. For example, the IFES Associate General Secretaries handle many staff matters that would otherwise come to the General Secretary.]

* As frequently as feasible, and no less than annually, the General Secretary should attend staff conferences so that he has first-hand interaction with his entire team. Only in the very largest movements may this be impossible. These contacts will be most fruitful if they include times for listening to staff as well as speaking to them. I well remember the timely exhortation of a staff person who said to me as a regional secretary, "When you come to visit us here, we are always going to meetings and involved in ministry. We need to have you just sit and interact with us, both individually and as a team."

* A simple way to inform staff of board activity and response may be to circulate copies of minutes of board meetings. If board members are reluctant to have this done, perhaps a summary can be circulated to staff. It may also be wise to send to staff copies of staff reports given to the board. This will help staff understand the basis on which decisions are made by the board. In a large move-

ment team leaders may be the only ones to receive the full
report with authority to share what they deem appropriate
with their teams. Notwithstanding, it is important that the
General Secretary communicate his own responses to both
pending and final board decisions. His interpretation will
assist the staff in becoming full participants in the life of the
movement.

Staff responses to information about board activity range
from "I can't be bothered. Just let me get on with my
work." to "Who voted 'yes' on that recent proposal?" With
wisdom and grace the General Secretary will be able to help
the entire movement respond constructively and suppor-
tively to one another. Student workers are not known for
quiet compliance. Information and openness are the finest
antidotes to distrust, and enable people of diverse backgrounds to work together in love.

Communicating with the Public

Any movement has various publics:
        churches, pastors,
            donors, potential donors,
                students, graduates, faculty,
                    university/college authorities,
                        parents,
                            and a host of others.
Each public has special interests that could be catered to.
But the time, money, skill and energy available are limited.
Therefore each movement must necessarily set priorities
and focus attention on the most strategic public sector.

Some means of communication reach many sectors of the
public at once. For example, if a staff person speaks in a
church meeting, he may be contacting not only church
people and the pastor, but also some graduates, students
who are either in the university or soon to enter, parents of

students already involved, faculty, and donors and potential donors. A newsletter which is mailed may reach not only those on the list of students and graduates, but other members of their families and churches. HIS magazine in USA has been instrumental in non-Christian students finding Christ, despite its prime editorial content being the Christian student on campus.

So what does that say to the busy General Secretary? Aim at your prime audience, and expect many other people to be influenced as well. Don't try to target all groups. Conserve your energy, and God will multiply your efforts.

What are the prime groups at which we should aim? That will be determined by your purpose and situation. Customarily the purpose of public information is to contact people who are going to be most responsive to your movement, either in prayer, participation on campus, or giving money. By experience and your knowledge of people who are already involved, you will probably discover that the most efficient groups of people to reach (who are already inclined to participate) are graduates of the movement, followed by Christians in the churches from which staff and student members come, Christian parents of students, and other churches either in university towns or whose young people tend to go to university.

In many nations the most effective beginning is to build a list of names and addresses of people who have been involved in the student movement. If the postal system is suitable, A SERIES OF NEWSLETTERS mailed periodically (customarily monthly or bi-monthly) will be the most efficient first step. In countries where the telephone is increasingly common and affordable, the list should include complete phone numbers as well. By making note of the school where people have been involved in the movement, it may eventually be possible to target information to them about the ministry at their school.

<u>Thus a basic list includes name, address, telephone, and school.</u> Once the graduates are married this listing becomes muddied unless separate listings are kept for each spouse. If and when your movement enters the computer age, this type of record keeping will be simpler.

Despite the effort involved, first-hand contact with people is superior to even the most effective newsletter. Where feasible, the General Secretary should encourage all board, staff, and volunteers to keep in personal contact with as many friends as possible. Sharing the names on the present list, and enlisting the help of all in adding contacts to it will be an extremely important and valuable exercise.

There are many other helpful suggestions that come out of experience in various nations. Some have been documented in writing. Check with leaders in older movements that share your cultural situation.

Note our Master's example as a communicator:

"I no longer call you servants, because a servant does not know his master's business. Instead, I have called you friends, for everything that I learned from my Father I have made known to you." (John 15:15)

8
SPIRITUALITY

An organization is an organization is an organization. Not so!

Although an IFES movement shares common characteristics with any human organization, several significant differences exist:

1. The personal religious beliefs of each core member must conform to the basis of faith.

2. The organization itself purposes to cooperate with God the Holy Spirit in changing people from the inside out. This transformation is not accomplished by even the most effective organization, but requires divine intervention.

3. The authority of the Bible (which we affirm in the Basis of Faith) affects the manner in which we conduct our common affairs as well as our personal lives. We are a worshipping community.

In this chapter we will be exploring some ways in which national movements can deepen the spiritual fellowship of those who work together in central administration.

Interacting with God

BIBLE STUDY AND PRAYER are two of the most common activities which distinguish a Christian movement from secular organizations.

1. In Bible study and Bible teaching we are learning from the Lord about all facets of our personal and group life and work.

2. In prayer we interact with God, expressing ourselves openly, both corporately and individually. Worship, for example, is one aspect of prayer which brings glory to God and renews all those who participate.

Now let's take a look at how leaders can enable a group to function together spiritually as well as organizationally.

Spiritually Alive Leaders

Even as an early British pastor (Robert M. McCheyne) said, "The greatest contribution I can make to my people is my own personal holiness," so each General Secretary or board/council chairman cannot give spiritual leadership without a living relationship with Jesus Christ. When a leader neglects his own walk with God, the entire Christian community suffers.

One of the great temptations of Christian leadership is to use the blessing of God upon the ministry as a measure of one's own walk with God. Let us be warned by Matthew's account (7:21-23) of Jesus' teaching when he says "On that day many will say to me, 'Lord, Lord, did we not prophesy in your name, and cast out demons in your name, and do many mighty works in your name?' And then will I declare to them, 'I never knew you; depart from me, you evil-doers.'"

Another temptation is to focus so intensely on the ministry while studying the Bible and praying, that one's own love for Christ and nurture of one's inner spirit are neglected. Although preparation for Bible study is refreshing, if one focuses only on the ministry to others, one may personally become dry and brittle. I find that praying the very personal prayers of the psalmists helps keep my own spirit worshipful and loving toward God and man.

Leaders must also be careful to keep their faith focused in God, rather than in the organization. Faith in the organization will eventually demoralize the entire team. Why does this happen?

Because leaders put programs before people. The desire to be a growing, successful organization is a noble aim, but if employees are treated as pawns rather than people, they may well experience burnout, feel that nobody cares, and/or sense the disrespect of their leaders.

Godly Policies

The godly leader will aim to fulfill the Biblical standards for Christian groups, and incorporate those guidelines into the basic operational policies of the movement. Since policies define the customary way of handling various situations throughout an organization, they need to be compared with Biblical standards, not only secular business and organizational practice.

A useful guideline: If the same question arises more than twice, it is time to consider making a policy.

To illustrate: It is common business practice in some cultures to fire an employee without explanation and to give little, if any, termination pay. The Christian principle of caring for people will include a careful review of the implications of such a move so that the employee and his family will be provided for. Some Christian organizations do not contribute to government funds which provide unemployment compensation until an employee finds another position. If this is the case, the leaders must be doubly careful to provide special counsel and assistance to those who are being terminated. The bonus of this practice is an increased sense of security among all those still employed. The Apostle Paul's letter to Philemon is a fine example of how a caring leader should express his concern for a former employee.

If your movement needs to establish uniform policies, 1) establish a small committee to do so, since the average General Secretary or board chairman will not have time to do a proper job; 2) ask them to check the policy handbook of neighboring IFES member movements for general guidance; and 3) insure that local government regulations are followed. [Government requirements vary from nation to nation, but in most cases religious groups must meet secular standards.]

Temptations Leaders Face
Those who focus their faith in the human organization rather than in the Lord often

1. trust their carefully made annual and long-range plans.
2. expect that careful organizing with backup plans will enable them to attain their objectives.
3. assume that large attendance at an event is the most important criterion of its effectiveness.
4. consider a 51% majority vote a clear indication of God's will for a decision.
5. use threats, manipulation, and trading of favors to attain and maintain control "for the good of the organization."
6. give or withhold money to control the organization.
7. use flattery and promises of future favors to control people.
8. resort to gossip and criticism to undercut others.
9. take credit for work really done by others.
10. equate financial prosperity with effectiveness and success.

Practicing Our Spirituality
As a traveling secretary for a student movement, I have noticed a striking correlation between the prayerfulness of a group and its spiritual vitality.

Although it is true that prayerFULness alone does not guarantee the presence of faith and blessing, prayerLESS-ness invariably leads to spiritual weakness, which manifests itself in preoccupation with business and organizational matters, petty bickering, and lack of trust in the living God.

What, then, is the place of prayer in our movements? If we focus on the national or center of the organization, it should be expressed corporately as well as individually. Even if each leader has a lively personal prayer life, the movement needs corporate prayer among:

> board members and spouses,
> central staff and spouses,
> board and staff together,
> staff leadership team,
> and throughout the movement.

Additionally, prayer support needs to be encouraged among graduates, churches, friends, family members of board and staff, etc.

Prayer by the Leadership Team

Although an historic ingredient in student groups has been the daily prayer meeting, the national meetings of the board/council and staff team have not always followed this fine example.

Here are some suggestions about how the spiritual life of the central leadership teams can be expressed:

1. Periodically (annually?) hold a RETREAT away from the office to which both board/council members and staff leaders are invited. Geographic considerations and size may make it necessary to hold several gatherings. Some movements find it wise to include graduates, friends and interested students as well. The schedule will naturally include prayer and Bible teaching/discussion.

2. Do not simply open and close each meeting with a perfunctory prayer. In council and staff meetings encourage prayer at regular intervals during the meeting:

> * before a decision
> * when you reach an impasse
> * when a special need comes to your attention

    * when you learn that God has graciously inter-
vened and you want to express thanks to Him
    * when electing board members or appointing or
terminating staff
    * when any member calls for prayer

Note: If in the past prayer has never been this vital a part of meetings, the leader will need to openly discuss the reasons why this approach is chosen. Some members may initially be afraid to participate. Be patient, they will eventually participate when they are ready. Avoid a round of prayer in which every individual in rotation is expected to pray. Spontaneous conversational prayer will gradually emerge without such rigid expectations. [Several member movements have published small booklets to encourage group prayer.]

3. Any member of a committee or small group should feel free to call for prayer when the Holy Spirit prompts them. This sensitivity needs to be cultivated and encouraged among members.

4. The same approach can be taken to the role of the Bible in leadership meetings. A perfunctory reading is usually unhelpful, but a presentation or discussion of at least a quarter or half hour can be very meaningful. Longer periods of Bible study, focused on an issue the group is facing, can be a most fruitful way of uniting and guiding the leadership team.

5. It is useful to remember that many board/council members do not have very many occasions to be ministered to by the staff. They are often giving tirelessly of their own time and energy, without input from the movement. Those staff who are gifted in Bible teaching and spiritual ministry should be invited to lead sessions at the meetings of the board/council or senior staff. That way some staff who lack administrative talents can contribute to the national

leadership and be affirmed in their ministry.

Staff Prayer Backing

It is easy to forget that each staff person is in the front lines of spiritual warfare and needs strong spiritual support. Here, from my own experience, is a concise list of ideas about developing a group of people who will pray regularly for a staff person, or board/council member:

1. Decide that you need a core of dedicated people who will pray regularly for you. It can be daily or weekly, as the Lord leads.

2. Pray that God will lead you to people whom He calls to this work.

3. Write a letter to those friends and acquaintances who seem to have a lively prayer life, openly sharing your desire for regular prayer support. Invite them to pray about it and either to respond to you or alert them that you will be contacting them by phone or when next in their vicinity.

4. Instead of a letter, you may wish to phone people who seem likely prospects. Beware of accepting their reply on the first call. Instead, I have found it wise to present the idea, ask them to pray about it, and then re-approach them for their answer in a couple of weeks. Using this delayed response, God has given our family several dozen people who have prayed regularly for us for several decades.

5. Be alert for students, friends, people who are specially blessed by your ministry, and churches who show a particular interest in your work. Ask them to consider praying regularly for you.

6. As an itinerant staff worker, I visited local pastors and asked them if they would give me the names and phone numbers of some of the praying people (including invalids and older people) in their congregations. By visiting these godly people, God provided many years of regular prayer

support for both the staff member and the local student group.

7. Communicate with those who have agreed to pray for you by means of a letter every month or two. Annual letters are NOT adequate to maintain the bond in most cases. If all are within phone range, you may wish to substitute the telephone. But I have found that even nearby friends find the letter with an occasional updated picture a helpful reminder.

8. From Vincent Craven of Canadian IVCF I learned that a postal card sent when traveling does a great deal to strengthen the personal tie with friends. If you have their names on a computer, print out the address labels, carry them with you, and you'll find it very easy to address your cards.

9. What should you write about?
    a. Share your own life and family.
    b. Share what you have been doing.
    c. Talk about your forthcoming schedule and some of the things you're facing.
    d. Don't simply talk about the people you're ministering to and their needs. These particular people are praying for YOU. A separate approach can be worked out for the student groups and other aspects of your movement.

National Movements Express their Godliness as They Are . . .

loving	praying	friendly
caring	studying	like-minded
affirming	witnessing	fair to all
rebuking	discipling	believing
exhorting	teaching	obeying
confronting	learning	praising

Guidelines for Christian Leaders

Not peace at any price.

[James 3:17: But the wisdom from above is FIRST pure, THEN peaceable, gentle, open to reason, full of mercy and good fruits, without uncertainty or insincerity.]

Not catering to selfish desire.

[Philippians 2:1-3: So if there is any encouragement in Christ, any incentive of love, any participation in the Spirit, any affection and sympathy, complete my joy by being of the same mind, having the same love, being in full accord and of one mind. Do nothing from selfishness or conceit, but in humility count others better than yourselves.]

Not by external pressure.

[I Peter 5:2,3: Tend the flock of God that is your charge, not by constraint but willingly, not for shameful gain but eagerly, not as domineering over those in your charge but being examples to the flock.]

Who is sufficient for these things?

As Paul says in II Cor. 3:5 "Not that we are sufficient of ourselves to claim anything as coming from us; our sufficiency is from God . . ."

9
GRADUATE FELLOWSHIPS

The Credibility of a Movement will be Determined by the Quality of Its Graduates

Students who participate in our movements inexorably march toward graduate status without reference to their progress as Christians. They might be "freshers" in Christ, but the academic world confers their degree and bids them farewell. Those who become Christians in their last years leave the student group without experiencing the richness of our discipleship programs for more than a short time.

Is it therefore valid to affirm that a movement's effectiveness is determined by its graduates? Yes, of course. Since our vision is to both PROCLAIM CHRIST and to MAKE DISCIPLES, we have a commitment to evangelize students at any stage of their academic work. Some will therefore be sent into their careers as young Christians; others will be mature in Christ even though novices in their vocation. Both levels can testify to the quality of our stewardship as IFES movements.

How can we insure that our graduates continue to grow in Christ and take their place in Christ's kingdom?

In the "Graduates" chapter we focused on the ministry of graduates to the student movement. In this issue we take a more careful look at how a movement can minister TO its graduates. On this subject we are especially indebted to Mr. Goh Keat Peng, until late 1989 General Secretary of the Graduates Christian Fellowship of Malaysia, a separate organization from the undergraduate work in that nation.

As General Secretary of the GCF Malaysia, Goh Keat Peng has had a great deal of experience in helping Christian graduates in a largely Muslim society.

What Do Graduates Need?
1. HELP IN TRANSITIONS
* from life as a student to life as a professional
* from student union and nearby church to a church
* from a close-knit small group to a church community with a larger age range
* from studying and exams to what may be a more routine workaday world

2. ADJUSTING TO NEW RELATIONSHIPS
* SOCIALLY: to a different circle of friends, since most graduates move to a new community
* in the FAMILY: assisting parents financially, dating and marriage, birth of children, etc.
* WORKPLACE challenges: finding a position, relationships with superiors, learning how to supervise others, developing professional skills
* WORLD VIEW formation: including understanding a Christian perspective on one's own professional ethical and moral standards; balancing work demands with family obligations; learning how to save, spend and give one's money;
* coming to terms with ONESELF: ambitions and aspirations; new awareness of one's emotions and vulnerabilities; applying one's faith in this new context.

3. FINDING ONE'S CHRISTIAN CALLING
* role in the local church and community
* response to the needy world--needing Christ, needing food, needing education, medical help, one's professional skills

* witnessing for Christ in one's profession
* developing and maintaining a rich devotional life

Who Should Help Graduates?

Ideally the LOCAL CHURCH picks up the nurturing roles that the student union has provided: Bible teaching, prayer groups, encouragement in witnessing, Christian fellowship, world view development.

Unfortunately, in many local communities there may be no local church or a very small fellowship. The graduate may be the only Christian at his professional level, particularly in many of our nations where the Christian community is a very small proportion of the society.

Furthermore, the graduate may be a threat to the leadership of the local congregation and kept at arms' length because of his broader experience and education. Or the opposite response may pertain: the graduate is overwhelmed with responsibilities heaped upon him in the church board, church school, choir, etc. He is always expected to be giving out; rarely taking in.

Where will He Find a Support System?

A GRADUATES FELLOWSHIP can be an ideal supplement to the ministry of the local church. In countries such as Malaysia, India, Nigeria and Colombia, the Graduates Fellowship is separately incorporated with its own General Secretary, but in close affiliation with the student movement. In most nations the graduates fellowship is still a fledgling, operating informally according to the local situation.

Britain has helped its graduates integrate their professions with their Christian faith through study groups in medicine, technology, education, etc. Some fine IVP publications have been formulated in these study groups, enabling the church at large to benefit from their insights.

Malaysia has challenged its graduates in larger cities to adopt graduates isolated in small communities for mutual encouragement. Sometimes those in rural settings come in to spend a weekend with graduates in the city, and at other times they welcome graduates from the metropolitan area into their own homes in the small communities. This kind of personal linkage is particularly important in societies where the Christian community is a small minority.

Both young and older Christians enter vocational situations that leave them vulnerable to many temptations and challenges to their Christian commitment. In the United States a "Marketplace" event is planned every few years to match students with Christian graduates who serve as mentors in various professions. This helps both students and graduates to integrate their professions and their faith.

Some Principles Learned in Malaysia

1. View the graduates group as a NECESSARY SUPPLE-MENT, rather than a distraction from local church work.

2. Keep the graduate ministry SPECIALIZED rather than general in nature.

3. DON'T DUPLICATE what churches and other para-church organizations are doing.

4. AVOID HOLDING REGULAR FELLOWSHIP MEETINGS such as many graduates experienced weekly in their student union. Integration into the local church will be delayed, and the meetings may grow stale over time.

5. Keep the ministry PROJECT ORIENTED, concentrating on pooling the resources of members. Both graduates and those ministered to will benefit as the strengths and talents of members are used.

Getting Started. Successful graduate work requires:

1. SPECIAL ATTENTION. An agreement at both senior staff and board/council levels that a graduate fellowship is important.

2. A PLAN OF ACTION. This is ideally developed by a small team of graduates who present a plan to the General Secretary and board/council for review and confirmation. Local models may already exist to help shape the plan, which should include recommended people, budget, and a timetable which includes check points for reporting on progress.

3. A DECISION to develop a graduates fellowship, stipulating the people and money that will be allocated to carry out the decision. (Graduates may rightly be expected to finance the work of their own fellowship.)

4. TEAMWORK. Student workers and graduates will need to work together to develop an effective ministry both to and by graduates.

5. SPIRITUAL FOUNDATIONS. Effective graduate work is a spiritual ministry which will involve prayer, Bible study, and humble Christlike service. The GCF Malaysia publicity folder quotes in bold type Luke 12:48: "Everyone to whom much is given, of him will much be required; and of him to whom men commit much, they will demand the more."

Members of GCF Malaysia are required to conscientiously sign the following declaration:

In becoming a member of this Fellowship I declare my faith in Jesus Christ as my Savior, my Lord and my God, whose atoning sacrifice is the only and all sufficient ground of my salvation; and I will seek both in life and thought to be ruled by the clear teaching of the Bible, believing it to be the inspired word of God.

Some Examples of Projects for Graduates
ADULT EDUCATION. Seminars/forums and courses in

continuing education for graduates. Subjects might include:
1. Christian family life relating to parents, marriage, parenthood
2. Issues of public interest
   the economy, unemployment and retrenchment
   brain drain
   colonialism
   ethnic relations
   Christian political ethics
   human rights
   corruption/public accountability
3. Christian community
   leadership skills
   church discipline
   spiritual gifts
4. Personal issues
   self-esteem
   shyness
   loneliness
5. Professional life
   work ethics
   work relationships
   motivation
   witness in the workplace
[Note: The graduate will often want to replicate in his local church what he learns in seminars of this kind, thus enriching his fellow Christians.]

Publications

PAPERS prepared for seminars may be suitable for publication and reach a wider audience. GCF Malaysia has published monographs on ethnic relations, freedom of religion, and emigration.

NEWSLETTERS keep members informed of activities and call their attention to resources which can help them in their leadership roles in church and society. GCF Malaysia has a monthly 8-page letter featuring a lead article on a Christian response to a current issue in their society, announcements of events, and reports and recommendations from graduates.

Study Groups

A study group may be the only place graduates receive assistance in developing theological reflection on issues significant in local and national society. As various individuals prepare and share study papers, the entire group benefits. Choosing a chairman who will stimulate involvement and challenge thinking ensures a profitable experience for everyone.

Career Expo

Twice each year the Malaysian GCF offers to recent grads and final year students a one-day (on a weekend) series of seminars led by experienced graduates. Separate rooms for each profession allow interaction and counseling on issues such as work ethics and difficult situations that challenge Christians in each field.

Christian Arbitration

The Bible exhorts us to settle differences among ourselves rather than resort to civil courts. GCF Singapore has set up a Christian arbitration service to facilitate such an approach.

Graduate Houses

Sometimes new graduates need accommodation while job hunting or when moving into a new position. Several graduates have pooled resources to rent a house, offering a free stay to new graduates until they obtain work. They then pay their way and in turn help meet the needs of others looking for employment. A graduate house can also be a base for Christian ministry and study.

Inter-Movement Conferences

In East Asia, graduates from various nations gather for mutual learning, encouragement, inspiration and friendship. Topics outlined in this issue form the program backbone for such events. Both region-wide and two-nation exchanges are useful.

Social Programs

Graduate groups can readily provide a place for singles to meet and get acquainted. Although the local church may already provide such occasions, an occasional GCF-sponsored social evening or outing adds cross-denominational interaction.

Graduate couples who open their homes provide a valuable ministry to single graduates. Interesting activities that appeal to graduates include watching a video together and then discussing personal responses.

Professional Services

Lay leaders of churches and full-time Christian workers can benefit when graduates offer their professional expertise to local churches. Here are some examples:
* computer programs with specific applications for church administration
* training in bookkeeping and simple accounting for honorary treasurers or church secretaries
* legal aid at reduced rates or free

CAUTION: Goh Keat Peng warns that such projects should not be an end in themselves, but aim to foster healthy social relationships, develop theological sense, and deepen concern for injustices so that graduates do something about them; e.g. to be salt and light in their world.

Organizational Structures

IFES movements have a wide variety of structures for graduates fellowships. Although there is no one best approach, Goh Keat Peng states that full time staff are essential for the graduate ministry to grow and fulfill its purpose. In larger, well-established movements that may be true.

But in a struggling smaller movement where volunteers carry a heavy part of the load, the graduate fellowship will usually be pioneered by volunteers who have helped formulate the plan, modeled a local version of a GCF, and committed themselves to implementing the plan.

Some final year students have been able to plan a graduates ministry with the help of their staff members, so that when they graduate they already have a commitment to making the plan a reality.

Since it is wise to develop a graduates fellowship in the early years of a movement's life, voluntary leadership by graduates will almost always be the first stage. By going through the steps outlined in the above section entitled "Getting Started", voluntary leadership should enable a movement to launch a graduates fellowship while it is still establishing its student work. After all, we have the Living God with us to call, enable and give the increase!

10
IFES AND THE CHURCH

Today the Church of Jesus Christ has been planted in every nation around the world. In some, it is publicly recognized, protected and helped by the government; in others Christians are forced to meet secretly at risk of imprisonment or death. But whether large or small, public or secret, the Church is the locus of Jesus Christ's Body on earth.

Is the Student Movement a Church?

Perhaps every staff person has at some time engaged in vigorous discussion with colleagues trying to answer that question.

A brief answer will include the following points:

1. While it is true that a) every person in leadership throughout IFES is a confessing Christian, and therefore a member of the church universal, and b) Jesus Christ has said that he is present whenever two or three meet together in His name, our student movements do not perform all of the functions of a local church. Baptisms, funerals, and weddings customarily lie outside the parameters of the student movement.

2. The student movement is primarily an evangelizing agency, whose members are involved for the few years they are in the academic world.

3. The participants are restricted to those who fulfill the academic requirements of educational institutions, whereas the church is open to people of all ages, interests and abilities.

4. Leadership is in the hands of the laity, which serves as an excellent training ground for future leadership in the local church.

Since the student groups are not a full expression of the body of Christ, it is appropriate that the student movement have a policy of encouraging each participant (student, staff, and council member) to participate in a local congregation.

This dual relationship is often a source of tension for student, staff and council members. Both local church and student movement are eager to have willing, skillful workers. Since students customarily represent the more talented members of a congregation, they are expected to give leadership according to their gifts. But the same gifts are often needed in the student movement.

How Do We Resolve this Tension?

Several basic understandings have been helpful in a number of our movements.

1. A student is best evangelized by his fellow students. The student has a unique opportunity to win colleagues who are studying the same subjects and facing the same challenges.

2. The church should be encouraged to consider their students "missionaries" to the academic world. If the church has this vision, they will pray for and encourage students in their campus ministry.

3. As with other missionaries, the church will recognize that it cannot monopolize all of the students' free time. Other people will pick up the responsibilities which otherwise might have been handled by the students.

4. When the student lives at a school away from his home, the congregation will follow him in prayer and interest that will include asking for reports of his ministry on campus. This will keep their prayers alive and reassure the student that he is an important part of the church.

5. As non-Christian students develop an interest in the Gospel, the church can both pray and extend friendship to the inquirers when they are invited to visit the homes of Christian students.

6. If the church is in the vicinity of the school, various social and spiritual outreaches can be planned in conjunction with the Christian students. Then when students become Christians, they already know a church where they can be nurtured. This is a most effective combination!

Summary

By teaching and modeling these attitudes, the churches and the student movement will become partners in reaching the academic world. Both will benefit, and in the long run, the church of Jesus Christ will be enlarged and strengthened immeasurably. The local church which has lent its students to ministry at school will find that not only have its students been trained in Christian ministry, but new converts have been added to God's Kingdom and the congregation.

INTERNATIONAL BONUS. In addition to all of the benefits mentioned above, churches with a missionary vision will find people from other nations right at their doorstep. The students from their congregation will find themselves studying with potential leaders from nations that are closed to conventional missionaries. As students bring their international friends home, and as the church welcomes them, they form one of the most fruitful missionary forces in the world.

Why? Because the experience of moving into a new culture makes international students much more open than their counterparts who remain at home.

Encouraging sidelight: During the 1980s Christian students from Africa studying in Russia and China have been used by God in evangelism and ministering to the church in those countries which were closed to traditional missions.

Staff and the Local Church

Staff members, including general secretaries, inevitably face the tension between church ministry and their work in the movement. From one point of view this is like other lay people, except that most staff are better qualified than other laymen for various tasks in the church. They are therefore in greater demand.

Because of this, it is wise for the General Secretary to establish policies governing staff involvement in the local church. In IFES, it is suggested that the staff limit themselves to one committee in the church. This has the salutary effect of forcing priority decisions, and gives the individual staff person a basis for refusing to be put on multiple committees and becoming diverted from his job with the movement.

For longer term staff, their role in the local church can help them broaden their ministries, particularly to other age groups. Gifts and skills that are not needed in the student work may otherwise lie dormant. The change of pace from working with young people can be refreshing and actually give exposure to perspectives that will help them prepare their students for life after college.

The church fellowship also provides the staff person with a circle of peers who are closer to his own stage in life. When a staff couple with young children participate in a small church group or church school class with other parents, they will be fellow learners, and not simply the up-front leader. Every person needs peers and a group to whom he is accountable, so that rebuke and encouragement can be received in a non-work environment.

But some will say that they have this kind of fellowship

on the staff team. That may be true when the staff live in close proximity. But with itinerant staff, it is the local church at his home base which serves as the long-term focus of his family and should also be a spiritual "home" for the itinerant himself.

This becomes critical when discipline is necessary. The itinerant supervisor of staff people will not be able to provide the complete pastoral care that staff need when facing special difficulties or moral temptations. Nor will the board/council nor its chairman be able to handle the pastoral care of the General Secretary. The local church is much better equipped for this ministry.

I have observed, for example, that on the few occasions when a staff person has faced the need for moral discipline, the movement has wisely consulted with the pastor of the staff person's local church and encouraged them to exercise Biblical discipline. A supervisor of the student movement may participate in pastoral care, but is rarely an adequate resource for all pastoral needs which his workers require.

Co-dependence between staff leaders and local congregations is in this sense very healthy, an expression of the caring and cooperation the human body demonstrates among its members. (I Corinthians 12)

The Movement and the Local Church

The General Secretary and Board/Council are well advised to make at least an annual evaluation of the health of relationships with local churches and student groups.

This can best be done by:

1. inserting an entry in the job description of each staff worker and volunteer which encourages them to develop relationships with churches;

2. teaching students to value and participate in local churches;

3. asking board/council members to cultivate relationships with churches on behalf of the movement (and include this in the job description for them);

4. insuring that the job description of the General Secretary includes setting up appropriate networks with the leaders of various denominations in the country.   This can be carried out by various members of the team, and they should know that this is expected of them;

5. at least annually having a standing board/council agenda item for evaluating church relationships. (In preparation for that, the staff and volunteers should be asked to give a status report on church relations in their territories.)

6. It will also be wise to evaluate the representation of various church bodies among staff and board/council members, to keep the movement inter-denominational.

7. All of the above should be watered with prayer, lest division or strife result from arbitrary action.

Help New Students

Encourage each local student union to gather names of entering students from the churches represented in their community. Those who are going to other cities can be shared with student groups in those areas, or collected centrally for distribution to staff and students in those cities. Problem: Some students from church youth groups shy away from Christian meetings when away at college. Solution: Students almost universally appreciate friendship which has no religious strings attached. Contacts should be genuine, not just based on invitations to Christian activities.

Interdenominationalism Has Its Hazards

Student ministry is most effective when it is not restricted to serving one church or church group. But many movements work in an environment of various church and para-church groups. Each has its own doctrine and practice which is customarily more restrictive than the student movement. Among the major differences which distinguish groups are the following: the mode and meaning of the sacraments of baptism, the Lord's supper, spiritual gifts, church government, and essential doctrines of salvation.

The IFES Basis of Faith outlines the beliefs expected of leaders in the student movements. The requirements of many denominations go beyond those essentials, or in some cases fall far short of them. When the leaders of a group of churches insist that their members only participate in activities sponsored by those in complete agreement with every detail of their own beliefs, an interdenominational relationship is thwarted. Students from such groups will need much love and understanding as they work through the conflict which they face if they cooperate with the student movement. The General Secretary and board/council should seek ways to open channels of communication with leaders in churches and denominations in order to assist students or junior staff who are facing this problem.

I like the report of Christian cooperation in Argentina as described in the October 1989 WORLD CHRISTIAN magazine: "Despite the presence of numerous denominations, evangelical churches in Argentina are operating in remarkable unity of spirit and purpose. In every major city there is an interdenominational ministerial association that promotes unity. One pastor explained, 'When the harvest is plentiful, it grows taller than the fences. And then it is impossible to know where one lot begins and the other ends. The harvest points to the Lord of the harvest. He owns the fields.'"

It is the same when God is at work among students: denominational barriers lose their importance. Our eyes are on our common Lord and His goodness.

Unbiblical Views

We also recognize that some denominations hold tenaciously to beliefs that contradict the Bible and conflict with the IFES Basis of Faith. They propagate doctrines which will lead students astray. In those cases we are obligated to teach and follow God's Word by limiting leadership to those who can unreservedly sign the IFES Basis of Faith. We also do not cultivate relationships with those denominations that propagate falsehood, though we pray and seek to win to Christ students of any religious or anti-religious persuasion.

When an official "State Religion" exists, special complications or benefits may result. Official religions vary so widely among nations that we are unable to deal specifically with them. Your IFES regional secretary and church leaders will be able to help you resolve these complications.

Local Church Domination

When only one church in the vicinity of a school has a minister who resonates well with students, the student union on campus may appear to be an extension of that church. How can we retain the openness of an interchurch fellowship without discouraging the majority of students who attend that church?

1. Continue to stimulate students in Christian outreach to people without respect to church affiliation.

2. Avoid making public announcements of church activities at campus events.

3. Raise the issue when talking with the student executive so student leaders will join in forging a satisfactory solution.

> Now to him who is able to do immeasurably more than all we ask or imagine, according to his power that is at work within us, to him be glory in the church and in Christ Jesus throughout all generations, for ever and ever! Amen. - (Eph 3:20, 21)

Terminology

"Para-church" is the term commonly used to describe the many specialized organizations that have sprung up in nations with a large Christian population. "Sodality" is introduced by Ralph D. Winter to distinguish Biblical and historic para-church agencies vs. "modality" for synagogue and diocesan frameworks. A useful Biblical/historical study, "The Two Structures of God's Redemptive Mission," is available from Wm. Carey Library Publishers, PO Box 40129, Pasadena, CA 91104 USA.

11
GROWING PAINS

Both a maturing child and a developing organization experience growing pains. In neither case are they a sign of abnormality. Rather, the pain is a sign that changes are occurring which require adjustments. If an organization ignores the pain, it will almost certainly find the warnings becoming more strident in their call for changes.

A Biblical Example
Acts 6:1-7 recounts the story of how the twelve apostles handled growing pains by straightforward action:

In those days when the number of disciples was increasing, the Grecian Jews among them complained against those of the Aramaic-speaking community because their widows were being overlooked in the daily distribution of food. So the Twelve gathered all the disciples together and said: "It would not be right for us to neglect the ministry of the word of God in order to wait on tables. Brothers, choose seven men from among you who are known to be full of the Spirit and wisdom. We will turn this responsibility over to them and will give our attention to prayer and the ministry of the word.

"This proposal pleased the whole group. They chose Stephen, a man full of faith and of the Holy Spirit; also Philip, Prochorus, Nicanor, Timon, Parmenas, and Nicolas from Antioch, a convert to Judaism. They presented these men to the apostles, who prayed and laid their hands on them."

"So the word of God spread. The number of disciples in Jerusalem increased rapidly, and a large number of priests became obedient to the faith."

Let's probe:

1. What was the specific growing pain?
2. Who spoke out about it?
3. What indicates that the complaint was justified?
4. How did the apostles involve the congregation in the solution?
5. How did they avoid allowing the pain to divert them from the main task?
6. What resulted from this corrective action?

Now notice the different activities which the apostles experienced as they handled the situation:

> listening
> judging, evaluating
> establishing priorities
> deciding
> calling people together
> publicly stating the problem
> recommending a solution
> delegating responsibility (choose 7)
> accepting the decision of the group
> prayer and laying on of hands

In this instance, a specific verbal complaint defined the problem. But not all growing pains should be allowed to develop to the point that a group complaint becomes necessary. When a movement is small, staff often work in isolation and have little opportunity to interact with others. They experience problems of various kinds, but have little opportunity to share them with colleagues. So no group complaint is possible. The General Secretary must be alert to needs of individual staff, and be quick to check out whether other staff members face the same problems. If

they do, the solution can be applied throughout the
movement.

Let's take a look at some of the warning signs which
indicate that some action needs to be taken to ease growing
pains.

Warning Signs
Staff welfare:
    months of overwork without relief
    salaries only partially paid
    burnout
    wives and children neglected
    surprise resignations
    no uniform vacation policy
    no reports; no response to reports
    rivalry and infighting
    uncertain job assignments
Central office functions:
    overdue bills
    late salaries
    piles of unanswered letters
    unread or unacknowledged reports
    lack of budgets or budgetary control
    General Secretary never in the office
    General Secretary always in the office
    field staff growth without office backup
    telephone lines always busy
    late expense checks
    donor receipts delayed
    board/council not kept informed
    staff recruits wonder if their application has been lost.

It is common for leaders of student movements to be so
deeply involved in ministry to students and staff that
administrative functions are neglected.

The converse may also be true: that conscientious leaders take care of the administrative functions, but neglect giving leadership to field staff and student groups. Most general secretaries come into the movement from field work, and thus resist tending to the office/administrative side of their responsibilities.

An added complication arises when a General Secretary, though willing, lacks the ability to handle administration. He may have great gifts of leadership and student ministry which qualify him to give overall leadership to the movement. But without attention to administrative functions, the movement suffers at every level. The warning signs outlined above begin to permeate the movement, the General Secretary becomes discouraged, the staff and board know that something must be done.

How Can We Handle These Growing Pains?

This month the editor has the privilege of sharing the experience of the Sveriges Evangeliska Student-och Gymnasistrorelse (SESG), movement in Sweden. For at least ten years, God has given that movement a stable leadership team with a successful division of responsibility.

In the following paragraphs, their General Secretary, Hans Lindholm, describes their situation and shares insights learned during the past decade.

An Overview of the Swedish Movement

Sweden is a rather complicated society. Even a Christian and independent movement must have many contacts with authorities and a wide knowledge of laws and regulations.

Sweden is also a country with old democratic traditions. Our model is very much built on consultation, committees, compromises. It is only during the last few years that trade and industry have asked for strong individual leadership. (We regard it as an American influence.)

SESG is, by IFES standards, an old, established, middle-sized movement with about 30 employees. This calls for a structure, finance and administration.

How SESG Coped with Administrative Needs
SESG was large enough before I became General Secretary to completely overload my predecessor. He was torn between different duties, until the movement found a new way of sharing leadership. Under this shared leadership, the General Secretary has responsibility for the theological and ideological leadership, while the Administrative Secretary assumes some of the functions formerly handled by the General Secretary. Let me describe how the functions are divided.

The Administrative Secretary
* is head of our office
* is responsible for agendas and minutes in board and executive committee meetings. [Our board is composed of 5 tertiary students, 4 high school students, and 5 "seniors."]
* is responsible for finances and budget
* coordinates the staff and leads them in matters of salaries, taxes, insurance. leaves of absence, holidays, sick lists
* is responsible to the Board and presents certain issues to them

The General Secretary
* is overall leader of the movement
* is responsible for the theology and ideology of the movement
* travels, speaks, and writes within the movement to uphold its policies and vision
* represents the movement in outward contacts

* supervises the staff and is responsible for their efficiency and welfare
* is responsible to the Board and presents certain issues to them

How Does it Work?

Hans writes, I know that some find the whole idea completely impossible, but the two of us have endured one another for ten years . . .

But the model has some necessary conditions: The two must be able to work together. They must have a mutual trust, so they don't end up competing for power. They must both have a spiritual understanding of the work. They must share a common direction of vision so they don't counteract one another. They must have a personal confidence so they can argue and yet leave tasks with the other. They must have natural and spiritual gifts that complete one another (again: not compete!).

In the IFES family there are, of course, many movements that are either too small or too large for this structure. And it may be that my co-worker Goran, who truly is a gift to me and to the movement (he doesn't know I'm writing this), is so special that general conclusions are dangerous. But my experience tells me that a similar structure could be worth considering in some movements, where the General Secretary needs somebody to share his burdens and where the work needs a balance between empathy and business, between theology and administration.

What Are Some Other Solutions?

JOB SPLITS

In a small movement it may be possible for field staff having administrative skills (bookkeeping, accounting, and handling conference registrations) and supervisory skills (serving as leader of a staff team) to perform these functions in addition to their regular student work. Although their own work with students should be reduced accordingly, this job split can spare the movement severe growing pains. As the movement develops, those tasks which grow into full-time jobs may then be assigned to a person skilled for the particular task.

In fledgling movements, the personal secretary to the General Secretary is the natural person to pick up various central office functions, since he/she is the only person regularly in the office. With support and training, a willing person in this role can relieve the staff of a surprising amount of detail.

VOLUNTEERS

In a small movement where administrative tasks are still part-time functions, volunteers have customarily been able to assist with various office duties. In one instance a housewife was able to give two or three hours five days a week to assist in handling mail opening, incoming checks, banking, and mailing receipts to donors under the supervision of the treasurer (also a volunteer). This enabled the General Secretary to travel freely and insured that proper care was given to financial affairs.

Volunteers may also help train and supervise junior staff workers, especially if they are working in a remote place. Long-term Christian faculty members who have been involved in the ministry have a wealth of experience that will benefit young staff members. Former staff workers and graduates can also contribute much support to staff, especially those who are new appointees. Each volunteer thus eases the growing pains caused by lack of local supervision or support.

HIRING OUTSIDE EXPERTS

In many countries it is possible at modest cost to engage an accounting firm to handle BOOKKEEPING and ACCOUNTING matters. Sometimes banks will do this for small businesses. It is important that this be overseen by someone on the board/council, such as the treasurer, or an employee with experience in financial affairs. Accounts need to be kept in balance and reports must be routinely submitted to the General Secretary, board/council, and government (where required). All bills should be o.k.'d by a qualified full-time employee who knows whether merchandise or services have been received. This check point cannot be delegated to an outside agency.

In some nations private agencies will tumble over one another in offering to assist in FUND RAISING. This kind of outside support must be carefully reviewed by both staff and board/council, with careful attention to financial terms, Biblical standards, and public image.

Creative Tension

Paper vs. people. Office vs. field.

The essential administrative problem in our movements often lies in the reluctance of leaders to invest resources in handling such mundane matters as money, paperwork, and reports. Those of us who are giving our lives in evangelizing and discipling students find it bothersome to keep records, write reports, account for money, and form policies. We are restless at a desk. Most student workers are interested in people. At considerable cost to professional advancement, we have chosen to give our lives in bringing students to Christ and helping them grow in Him.

Yes, that is the proper first priority.

But without adequate administrative support, a student movement will fade away. Staff will be forced to leave because salaries are behind, or they are overworked, or

they have no one to help them resolve conflicts with colleagues. Students will fail to attend conferences because the announcements were late. Donors will stop giving because their gifts have not been acknowledged.
Pray-ers will fail to pray because the prayer guide has been discontinued.

What is happening? The network which enables people to learn how they can support and cooperate with one another has broken down. Members lack encouragement because they have no way of learning whether their contribution is worthwhile. Administrative support
is not optional: it is a God-given necessity.

Fortunately, many of our movements have found people who are called to work in administrative support roles. Usually they must put in long hours with little public recognition. Letters and phone calls dealing with a wide array of questions keep them enmeshed in details that other people prefer to avoid. But God has given them a call to this work and they keep serving the entire movement month after month.

Demonstrate Your Appreciation

If your movement is large enough to have administrative staff, how are you showing your appreciation?
* Do you remember to thank them?
* Do you share what God is doing in the lives of students when you talk with them?
* Have you ever thought of sending them a friendly postcard?
* At holiday time, do you think of remembering them with a box of sweets, or whatever people in your culture particularly enjoy?
* Have you thought of giving administrative staff reduced rates at conferences? . . . or even a free week with their family at a student event?

If board/council, general secretaries and field staff remember to affirm the administrative team, they will probably find it much easier to fill those positions with called, qualified people!

12
PEOPLE

Among Christians it is commonly accepted that people are more important than things. We have learned this from our Lord who raised the value of a human being beyond our fondest dreams when he left heaven and became human himself. Astonishingly, he demonstrated through his death on the cross that humans are so valuable that they are worth dying for. That is how we all have finally found our peace in the universe: redeemed by the Creator God and welcomed as His beloved sons.

Those of us in Christian leadership have the privilege of PROCLAIMING this wonderful truth as we seek to win students in our schools, colleges and universities. But more than that, we have the task of WORKING OUT in our fellowships how God wants people of such great value to be treated. Surely if each individual member of our staff and board/councils is of such great value to God, some very special arrangements ought to characterize our relationships.

One of the primary implications will surely include better people attitudes in Christian fellowships than in organizations whose leaders do not understand the Gospel. Rather than our looking to secular agencies to determine people policies, it should be normal for us to search the Scriptures and observe how other Christians handle people relationships. The great care which Jesus demonstrated toward people of all kinds is our model for our fellowships. Unfortunately among Christian fellowships in various parts

of the world there are many situations which contradict Jesus' model. One can observe such common problems as:
* overworked staff;
* hurting workers who have no one to encourage them;
* families who are neglected;
* underpaid workers, even to the extent that children of some workers are undernourished;
* burn-out from long service without refreshment;
* arbitrary decision-making without consultation;
* conflict among staff which is ignored by supervisors, etc.

Why Is This So?

A few recurring causes include:

1. Lack of communication about the real situation, either through fear of disapproval, unrealistic idealism, or failure to listen to complaints or take them seriously;

2. Preoccupation with tasks to be done, so that the welfare of colleagues is ignored;

3. A stoical (austere) attitude by workers who ignore the price which their families are paying for their dedication;

4. Dispassionate board/councils who do not understand the pressures of poverty endured by staff;

5. Inexperienced and overworked leaders who have no energy left to care for their colleagues;

6. Leaders who are so concerned about fulfilling their own public ministry that they neglect the needs of their colleagues;

7. Leaders who feel that administration is second-class ministry and thus ignore or neglect the care of people on their team.

What Can be Done to Rectify These Problems?

When any member of either the staff or board/council becomes aware of a need in a fellowship, it is appropriate for that person to assume that God has given him/her this gift of wisdom. And to what purpose? Surely not for gossip or criticism, but rather to build up the body of Christ.

It is surprising how often people feel uneasy about something, but fail to identify the problem. Then an insightful person verbalizes an unhealthy condition that exists, and others confirm its truth. At that point the body of Christ can begin to work together in clarifying and resolving the problem. The healing process is underway.

Not infrequently someone outside the staff and board/council may be the first to identify a problem. The Holy Spirit moves whomever He chooses, and it is important for leaders to listen to truth whatever its source. So we have pointed out the first two things we can do to rectify problems:

1. Identify the problem (This can be done by anyone, inside or outside the fellowship.); and

2. Listen carefully to those who have identified the problem, in order to clarify and test its validity.

At this point, leaders in the fellowship will need to identify the process by which corrective action should be taken: which person(s) should work on the resolution and when and how they should proceed.

A Better Way

The process above is appropriate for solving problems that have occurred, but is there not a better way? Isn't there preventive action that can be taken? Yes. Many people problems can be avoided with policies and procedures which our movements (and other sectors of society) have found useful in building healthy relationships in a fellowship. Although we cannot take a careful look at all of them, a few basic ideas will get us started.

1. THE BOARD/COUNCIL MAKES A COMMITMENT TO ITS PEOPLE.

It is appropriate for a board/council to take its people seriously. Few, if any, of our movements have buildings or a large formalized hierarchy to give status or stability. Our people are the core of all we do; without competent board/council members and staff people the work of IFES movements evaporates.

Some organizations in their overall purpose statement include an entry that publicly recognizes the importance of its people in fulfilling its objectives. The by-laws of one of our movements state:

"We realize that while organization is necessary, God's method is men empowered by the Holy Spirit in the service of the Lord Jesus Christ. We acknowledge, therefore, our complete dependence upon God. These by-laws have been developed in order that the men and women serving with the Fellowship may function most effectively."

2. THE POLICIES OF THE ORGANIZATION ADDRESS THE WELFARE OF ITS PEOPLE.

Although a movement builds and refines its personnel policies throughout the life of the organization, many useful ideas can be incorporated from the start by learning from others. Below is a list of some of the categories which need to be addressed:
* qualifications for employment
* recruitment and screening procedures
* orientation and training of employees (both field and office)
* job descriptions
* supervision of employees
* reporting
* evaluation and review
* promotion or transfer

* fund raising expectations
* remuneration
* expense accounts
* benefits (health & life insurance, pension, holiday & vacation, sick leave, moving expense, etc.)
* grievance procedure
* termination, retirement

3. THE LEADERS OF THE ORGANIZATION ACTIVELY CARE FOR THEIR PEOPLE.

Even with the very best policies, it is still possible for people in an organization to be neglected. This becomes evident when within a larger fellowship people in one area feel tremendously supported, whereas those in another area feel abandoned. The same policies are in place in both areas. What is the difference?

Almost invariably, the difference lies in the ATTITUDE and ABILITY of the supervisor. In one area the supervisor expresses his love, care and concern in ways that meet team members' needs. In the other area, people feel neglected, unsupported, and perhaps even think that their leader is antagonistic to them. They find that they must invoke written policies in order to receive fair treatment. Sometimes this negative climate is exacerbated by the supervisor taking credit himself for work done by supervisees, without acknowledging the hard work done by his team. The self-centeredness or insecurity of the leader keeps him from providing the encouraging climate which every worker deserves.

PARTIALITY is another characteristic which destroys morale. If certain people are given favored treatment, others on the team may find it difficult or impossible to avoid resentment. In some instances it is possible for a leader to be unaware of the partiality he is showing. In either case, the offended people need to prayerfully confront the leader and encourage him to treat everyone alike.

One of the special instances where partiality may be a problem is when two members of the same family work in the same area. If, for example, a wife is employed and supervised by her husband, people who work beside the wife may feel that they are at a disadvantage. To avoid this problem, it is wise to set a firm policy that two individuals from the same family may not work in the same department. Although some cultures may have built-in mechanisms which avoid this problem, the wise leader will check with his own supervisor before hiring a family member to serve under him.

Ten Simple Ways to Ruin Morale

1. Don't respond to reports sent by supervisees.

2. Ignore the questions asked by your supervisee in his report.

3. Don't return phone calls from those who report to you. Let them know that other people are more important to you.

4. Assume that your supervisee doesn't need help unless he asks for it.

5. Share confidences, even though you've promised confidentiality.

6. When visiting a supervisee, spend all of your time together in ministry to others.

7. Don't take the time to inquire into the welfare of the supervisee's family, and certainly never take the time to talk with the spouse or children.

8. Point out every mistake made by your supervisee, and never compliment him in public.

9. When with your supervisee, don't ask questions, but dominate the time by doing most of the talking.

10. When someone outside the movement criticizes a staff person, assume that the staff person is wrong and quickly accuse him of the failure.

Note: Although the relationship of the board/council to the General Secretary is less intimate, the above principles also apply to the relationship between the council chairman and the General Secretary. A caring relationship is always appropriate between Christians.

What are Some Basic Rules in Wholesome People Relationships?

1. Each person is entitled to a clear statement of his task.

2. He must have the authority to carry out the job assigned.

3. He deserves the orientation and training necessary to equip him for the task.

4. He can expect to be provided with the resources necessary to do the work, including payment for expenses incurred as well as appropriate equipment and facilities.

5. He has the right to know what his superiors think of his performance.

6. He is entitled to an adequate wage.

Some Brief Comments on the Above:

Although we could devote an entire chapter to each of the above, let us look at a few key aspects.

1. A clear statement of the task is usually called a "JOB DESCRIPTION" or "POSITION DESCRIPTION." Sometimes this is several pages long with many details. Customarily, and preferably, an adequate job description covers one typewritten page.

It is wise to use a suggested job description as part of the material given a prospective employee. This will give him a general idea of what will be expected if he accepts the job. Once the employee has worked at the job for a few months, it is often wise to review the job description and make mutually acceptable adjustments which reflect the realities of the job as well as the skills and abilities of the worker.

A job description will:
* define the purpose of the job
* indicate to whom the person will report
* describe in general the various aspects of the task.
* Clerical jobs will often have a more detailed outline than campus ministry assignments.

A job description may:
* define the expectations for the personal spiritual-devotional life of the worker, e.g. daily quiet time, Bible study, church attendance, etc.;
* outline the kinds of personal and family relationships expected of a Christian worker;
* establish a standard of moral conduct by reference to Biblical passages;
* outline the geographic parameters of the worker's territory; etc.

[Samples of job descriptions may best be procured from other movements in your own cultural milieu, or your IFES regional office.]

2. AUTHORITY to do a task is given by the person's supervisor. The supervisor customarily is given RESPONSI-BILITY for the task, with authority himself to DELEGATE that authority to others who will help him do the work. A few basic principles of delegation are all we have room to mention:

a. Delegation will often be progressive, both in scope and time. A new employee may have limited authority because of inexperience. But as he matures in the job, his authority may increase accordingly.

b. Delegation of authority does not mean delegation of responsibility. The supervisor still holds responsibility and will be held accountable for the work by his own supervisors.

c. Once a supervisor has delegated authority, he wisely allows those reporting to him to keep that authority rather than taking it back whenever he chooses.   Whimsical interference by supervisors is frustrating to those assigned the job and makes them insecure and unsure of just what they are to do.   A delegated task should remain in the hands of the supervisee unless and until his performance indicates he is unable to perform satisfactorily.   Handling such a situation in a godly manner requires people skills of the highest calibre.

13
PASTORAL CARE

I can't remember anyone ever disagreeing with the phrase "No man is an island." And we know from experience that we are dependent upon other believers to help us grow in the Christian life. Most of us have strong affection for those who have nurtured us in the Christian faith.

Long ago the Apostle Paul clearly summarized this in his letter to the Ephesian Christians (4:11-13): "It was he (Christ) who gave some to be apostles, some to be prophets, some to be evangelists, and some to be pastors and teachers, to prepare God's people for works of service, so that the body of Christ may be built up until we all reach unity in the faith and in the knowledge of the Son of God and become mature, attaining to the whole measure of the fullness of Christ."

Healthy IFES movements have people at staff, student, and board/council levels who use their gifts to minister to one another. In fact, one of the main gifts which the General Secretary needs to exercise is that of pastoral care: staff members need an understanding ear and words of advice and encouragement; students come up after a talk and request counsel; even graduates find many situations where they value the input from the General Secretary and staff.

Now comes the tough question: who pastors the General Secretary? To whom can the General Secretary turn for advice, counsel, encouragement or rebuke? Has your movement seriously and straightforwardly made provision for the pastoral care of your General Secretary?

IFES international provides some pastoral care through its regional secretaries and a few traveling staff who not only visit nations periodically but also convene annual or biennial conferences to assist general secretaries. But is this adequate? Many general secretaries have expressed a need for additional pastoral help.

Who Should Provide this Pastoral Care?
A. FOR EMPLOYEES IN FIELD & OFFICE

The General Secretary should insure that this kind of care is given each member of the staff and office teams.

1. He himself should give this kind of pastoral care to those who report directly to him.

2. The job description of members of his immediate team should include the pastoral care of those under them.

PERSONNEL POLICIES of the organization should be developed to insure that proper pastoral care is given to all employees. A generic entry in a supervisor's job description which simply states "to provide pastoral care to all those who report to him" is not adequate to insure that proper care is given. More detailed policies need to be explained in a manual for supervisors. This will help insure uniform treatment at all echelons of the movement. [Check with older movements in your region if you want samples of policies others have worked out.]

B. FOR THE GENERAL SECRETARY

The board/council is then the only remaining part of the organization which can provide pastoral care for the General Secretary. But several questions immediately arise:

1. How can a GROUP of people who meet periodically provide adequate pastoral care?

2. Can we expect the average chairman of the board/council to have the gifts needed to provide pastoral care?

3. Can the board/council expect that the senior staff of the movement will pastor the General Secretary?

4. Will the pastor of the General Secretary's local church automatically provide this care?

5. Or is one of the prerequisites for selection of a General Secretary that he can function without pastoral care?

The answer to all of the above will surely be "NO!"

Some Kinds of Help which Leaders in Christian Organizations Need

A clear JOB DESCRIPTION which they review periodically with their supervisor.

A definite plan of ministry emphasis (PRIORITIES) for the year ahead.

A regularly scheduled REVIEW and EVALUATION of his own work, not just that of the entire movement.

A plan for personal enrichment through SPIRITUAL DIRECTION, learning NEW SKILLS and/or CONTINUING EDUCATION.

Someone with whom to cross-check his daily, weekly, monthly and annual PATTERNS OF WORK.

A definite commitment for an ANNUAL VACATION, completely away from work.

A loving, yet candid, discussion with a trusted friend who will help him and his wife evaluate the WELFARE OF HIS FAMILY.

An annual review of SALARY BENEFITS, in light of personal and family needs.

A periodic update of his EXPECTED LENGTH OF SERVICE, expressed in written format after discussion with his board/council; e.g. for 2, 3, 5 or more years.

How, Then, can a Board/Council Handle Its Responsibility?

Even though a board/council may have felt that pastoral care of the General Secretary has been well handled by the chairman of the board/council, how carefully has this been evaluated? Is this conclusion drawn from comments the chairman has given the board? From a lack of complaints from the General Secretary?

Those who are acquainted with needs of general secretaries discover

1. that they are often reluctant to open their hearts to busy board/council members;

2. that sometimes problems surface only when severe damage and pain have been endured;

3. that even the most committed board members fail to see the pressures which a General Secretary and his family are enduring;

4. that sometimes a General Secretary quietly resigns without ever revealing the true reasons for his departure.

So what can a board/council do? Several things can bring long-term blessing:

1. The board/council should discuss together and agree that pastoral care of the General Secretary is too important a responsibility to ignore. [See chapter 12, "People"]

2. A small sub-committee of the board/council could be established to review the whole matter and work with the present General Secretary in developing a plan to address the pastoral care aspects mentioned above in "Some kinds of help . . ." Graduates or board/council members whose professional life is in the field of personnel relationships may be very helpful members of such a sub-committee.

Here are some clues that may make the job of the sub-committee easier:

1. If your movement or a neighboring movement has already developed personnel policies for employees, each entry will be a useful outline to guide your discussions. Surely general secretaries will need the same categories of care which other staff require!

2. Talk with your IFES regional secretary about the ways in which various movements in your region handle the

pastoral care of their general secretaries.   Understandably, both positive and negative examples will emerge.

3. If your movement already has personnel policies for field and office staff, the main task of the committee may simply be to determine what, if any, additional entries are needed by the General Secretary.   Look especially for ways of helping someone who bears the many-sided pressures of every aspect of the work, both inside and outside the movement.   For example, I have just visited with a General Secretary who lives in a nation where the government has recently imprisoned certain Christian leaders and is in the process of increasing pressure on Christians.   Surely this is a time when the General Secretary needs specialized pastoral care--beyond that of other staff.

Once pastoral care functions are clearly defined and agreed upon, the next task is to determine WHO will provide the care.

Will one member of the board/council be able to handle all aspects?

Can a committee of three people provide pastoral care?

Who will decide how to divide up the pastoral functions, if more than one person is responsible?

There is no single best answer to the above questions. The skills and personalities of the caring people will affect the answers, as will the outlook of the General Secretary. Whatever assignment is made, it is important that the General Secretary be CONSULTED and CONTENTED with the arrangements that are worked out.

There is one important distinction to keep in mind: the board/council membership and leadership change periodically, so that any pastoral care assignments carried out by Board/council members must be reviewed annually. It may be wise to continue an active personnel committee so this review is given priority.

How will the Entire Board/Council Review the Effectiveness of Pastoral Care in the Movement, and of the General Secretary in Particular?

1. By insuring that at least once each year those who are assigned to give pastoral care to the General Secretary give a report to the board/council, with the General Secretary present. The General Secretary should be encouraged to affirm, correct, or amplify the pastoral report.

[It is important that the relationship between the pastors and the General Secretary be open so that such an exercise is done comfortably with both pastors and General Secretary present. If members of the board/council desire a private session without the General Secretary present, the content of that meeting should be revealed to the General Secretary by those assigned to be his pastors, even when the content of the discussion may have raised questions about whether he should be retained in his position. Closed sessions of the board can be very threatening to a General Secretary. If he is uncertain about whether the board/council is satisfied with his job, he will not perform well, and the unity and freedom of the Holy Spirit in the movement will be hindered.]

2. By asking the General Secretary to report to the board annually on the way in which pastoral care is being given and received in the movement.

3. By providing funds for training courses for supervisors to assist them in adequately caring for their staff.

Neglected Pastoral Care Issues

Although we have focused on the pastoral care of the General Secretary, there are other recurring needs which movements too often overlook. Here are some that merit careful consideration:

PAY SPECIAL ATTENTION TO THESE
1. The welfare of wives, especially of itinerant workers.
2. Meeting the emotional and educational needs of children of staff.
3. The long-range vocational future of long-term staff. (What happens if they leave the movement? . . . or if they stay?)
4. The tendency to neglect one's own personal needs which results in "burn-out" among our many conscientious staff.
5. The painful and sometimes thoughtless termination of staff.
6. The lack of encouragement and appreciation given staff.
7. Too large a job assignment without supervision to break it into manageable proportions.

Although in this chapter we haven't space to adequately discuss each of the above, let's take a look at the question of the needs of wives of workers, since too often their voices are never heard beyond the confines of their own homes or hearts.

The Christian Worker's Wife
The Apostle Paul's words in Ephesians 5:25-27 give incredibly high priority to wives: "Husbands, love your wives, just as Christ loved the church and gave himself up for her to make her holy, cleansing her by the washing with water through the word, and to present her to himself as a radiant church, without stain or wrinkle or any other blemish, but holy and blameless."

Does this exclude Christian workers? Never! Instead, they of all saints ought to set the example by giving themselves up for their wives, just as the Lord gave Himself for the church.

Unfortunately, the spirit among Christian workers too often means that both husbands and wives give themselves up for "the work", and the husband too easily forgets to give his wife the priority which Christ demonstrated.

Giving his wife priority will mean:

1. carefully listening to his wife,
2. observing her unspoken concerns,
3. asking questions to discern her outlook and opinions,
4. spending time with her alone,
5. taking over her tasks so she can get out of the home and be refreshed,
6. putting his own outward ministry second to her needs,
7. creatively planning ways to rid her of stains, wrinkles, and any other blemishes which he may learn about.

Many men are unaware of the pressures which their loyal, uncomplaining wives face day after day, month after month. Just a few days ago the wife of a longer term worker shared her struggle with her husband's return from a ministry trip. "He has had these exciting encounters with students, graduates and staff and is eager to share them. But I have been home with the children, no adults to interact with, and all I want when he returns is for him to take over and give me a rest from the demands of the home and children. I find I'm not even able to be interested in his adventures at that point." And many wives of Christian workers agree. They don't have the resources both to care for a growing family alone, and also provide a good sounding board for the husband when he first returns. That moment may well come later when the wife has had a chance to be refreshed and renewed in spirit.

But more than that, wives of workers in many movements are struggling with a very low income which adds a great deal of pressure to shopping and often means a less-than-adequate home. In almost every case her resources are far less than those either her or her husband's classmates enjoy as graduates. The same disparity usually exists between the lifestyle of the members of the board/council and General Secretary.

It goes without saying that all members of the supporting community need to be doubly sensitive to the needs of the wives of workers in all levels of our movements.

14
EVALUATION

How is the work going?

If you are a GENERAL SECRETARY, you will probably be able to answer that question in a variety of ways, varying from a) "Great! We've just had our best national conference in memory.", to   b) "We're facing some severe struggles right now, even though outwardly our work looks good."

Which is correct? There may be an element of truth in both answers, though they appear to be contradictory. The answer given will depend upon who asks the question, and when.

If you as a BOARD/COUNCIL MEMBER ask that question of your General Secretary, how are you going to know whether you're being given an "a" type answer or a "b" type answer? If you fail to probe with follow-up questions, you may learn only too late that the decisions you've made as a board/council member have been based on glossy comments rather than tough facts.

In this chapter let's take a more careful look at how we go about evaluating the work God has given us, with special focus on the ways in which Board/Council members can insure that they are gaining an understanding of how the work is really going, including the facts which may be tough and embarrassing.

Evaluation at Its Best

1. VALID INFORMATION   Some of us know well the saying "A person's judgment is only as good as his information." I, and many others, have found that statement true in various aspects of life, including decision-making as a parent, manager, council member and voter.   Gathering accurate information is not easy, but it is foundational to valid evaluation of a situation. Those with children know how far apart two viewpoints can be when a disagreement arises.   Careful probing is essential before a parent can discover what really happened. Likewise a proper evaluation of the student movement requires more than casual listening.

2. CLEAR GOALS   A second vital ingredient in adequate evaluation is a clear statement of purpose. What are we aiming to accomplish? The information we gain must be viewed in the context of what we intend to do. Even if we have an accurate picture of what has happened in our movement, the evaluation of whether it is good or bad will depend upon how it coincides with our aims.

If we have our largest conference ever, is it automatically our best? That all depends upon what we aimed for. Was having a large attendance our main aim? Then we have accomplished our goal. Was our objective to teach students that Jesus should be first in their lives? Then a completely different evaluative grid should be used.

3. COMPARATIVE DATA   Although in common parlance "comparisons are odious," a very useful evaluative tool is to compare performance this year with last. While it may be offensive to compare one student union with another, or one area with another, it is often helpful to measure the same group's performance today vs. yesterday, this year vs. last year.

4. CONNECTIONS   Valid evaluation must include a proper understanding of causal relationships wherever possible. To what extent did the efforts of staff enable this success or lead to this failure? What part did the work/ prayers of student leaders have in the success or failure of this project? How did the money given or not given for scholarships contribute to the success or failure? To what

extent did board/council members contribute to the suc-
cess/failure of this particular event?

Establishing connections may be the most difficult part of
the evaluative process, and must be done prayerfully with
great humility and caution.   But it is nevertheless an
important element in adequate evaluation. I can remember
times when the staff team has been downhearted because
a conference drew fewer students than expected.   Their
disappointment colored their ability to see and rejoice in all
God had done, which ultimately led to revival in several of
the student unions. Several months later everyone agreed
that the impact of that conference exceeded other larger
events over which there was much greater rejoicing
initially.

Even though the Bible tells us that "man looks at the
outside, but God looks at the heart," we must endeavor to
let our evaluation penetrate the surface and judge as God
judges. An interesting vignette which should encourage us
is found in 2 Chronicles 19:5-7:

> Jehoshaphat (King of Judah) appointed judges in the
> land, in each of the fortified cities of Judah. He told
> them, 'Consider carefully what you do, because you
> are not judging for man but for the Lord, who is
> with you whenever you give a verdict. Now let the
> fear of the Lord be upon you. Judge carefully, for
> with the Lord our God there is no injustice or
> partiality or bribery'.

Today, as well, we have the lord with us through the
Holy Spirit, who helps us evaluate (judge) in the fear and
wisdom of the Lord.

Having pointed out four aspects of evaluation, let's take
a look at how a movement can assess the health of the
work. Obviously the staff and board/council will need to

work closely together, since each contributes its own unique perspective to the evaluation.

What Sources of Information are Available to Board/Council Members?

FORMAL:

1. Routine reports presented at board meetings which may be either verbal and/or written. They will customarily include information about activities of leaders, major events, financial data, major personnel changes. These routine reports may be given by the General Secretary, other employees, or chairmen of committees of the board/council.

2. Special reports requested by board/council, which may be presented by chairmen of council committees, members of staff, or outside advisers.

3. Printed publications of the student movement which are distributed to the general public. It is wise for all board/council members to be placed on the general mailing list so they will know what friends of the student movement are being told.

INFORMAL:

1. Conversations with
   * fellow board/council members
   * the General Secretary
   * staff members
   * students (leaders, members of Bible study groups, people who have just attended their first meeting, etc.)
   * pastors, faculty, parents of students involved, or even your own children who may be involved in a Christian union.

2. Articles in newspapers or periodicals which comment on an event in the life of the movement.

3. A wide variety of other sources of information which cannot be controlled and are quite unpredictable.

When formal and informal sources of information harmonize, a movement will customarily enjoy a good relationship between its administration and board/council. Difficulties arise when the formal and informal conflict, especially when the informal information is negative. For example, when a member of a board/council has just read and heard a glowing report about the condition of the movement, he will be greatly concerned if someone tells him he perceives a serious difficulty in a certain part of the movement.

What Formal Reports will Enable Members of the Board/ Council to Assess the Condition of the Movement?
FINANCIAL
Board/council members will probably need no prompting to inquire about the financial health of the movement. Those with business backgrounds will expect to hear about income, expenditures, and how they balance out and compare with budget. In a small struggling movement, a question on everyone's mind is "Have the staff been paid on time?" And close behind it will be "Are we paying our bills on schedule?" Well and good! A board/council should be vitally concerned about the financial health of the entire organization. See the chapter on "Money" for further information.

ORGANIZATIONAL
Each movement will need to establish its own measures of organizational effectiveness. Ideally each of the major objectives of the movement should be measured. Categories might include entries such as:
Student groups:
  * number of groups in the entire movement
  * average number of participants per group
  * % of student groups sending leaders to training conferences

* number of students becoming Christians
* number of students engaged in Bible study groups
* number of students who participate in outreach to those from other cultures
Staff:
* number of schools each staff member is caring for
* additions to staff this period
* deletions from staff, and reasons why
* training programs for staff and their effectiveness
* morale of staff (This is difficult to objectify, but should be attempted. Some clues are found in staff turnover, unity among staff, eagerness of recent graduates to apply for staff service.)
* positive impact of staff on student groups. (Another aspect which is difficult to measure in individual cases. But ability to attain agreed objectives and overall growth and development of student leadership in a staff member's territory give some indication.)
Events:
* objectives attained
* objectives missed and why
Relationships:
* attitudes toward the movement and by the movement within a) the academic community; b) the Christian community; c) donors; d) any other entities important to the movement.
* attitudes between the staff and board/council

ADMINISTRATIVE
Although there is often overlap between organization and administration, it is helpful to retain the distinction. The following entries exemplify the kind of measurements that should be considered.
Personnel:
* availability and calibre of new recruits for staff

* quality of orientation and training of new staff
* care of long-term staff
* policies for vacation, health insurance, sick leave, sabbaticals, pensions, etc.
* welfare of staff families, including education of children

Management:
* nurture and training of staff
* adequacy of supervision
* adequacy of refreshment and training programs for staff
* team spirit and morale

SPIRITUAL

Churches and Christian organizations lack a neat and universally accepted method of evaluating the spiritual effectiveness of their work. Some will simply assess the number of people who have professed faith in Christ during a certain time frame; others will carefully tabulate attendance at different meetings; still others rely largely on the level of enthusiasm which the staff leader exhibits while he speaks to the council. There are even those who equate financial health with spiritual well-being. While it is true that all of these may reflect some aspect of health in the movement, none of them alone measures spiritual health.

An adequate indicator of spiritual effectiveness will necessarily be tied to the objectives of the organization. Leaders of a movement can outline their measures of success at the time they lay their plans. This exercise will help them clarify objectives and the conditions they expect to exist when the plan has been carried out. For example, if a conference is held to help students establish investigative Bible studies, one of the criteria of effectiveness will be the number of studies that subsequently are established.

Even more detailed evaluation is carried out in some movements, e.g. how many students become Christians through those studies. Wisdom is required to know how much energy to put into detailed evaluation, since it can lead to frustration and endless research which is counter-productive.

How to Keep Evaluations Healthy
1. TRUST YOUR STAFF. Unless the movement is very small and the staff team inexperienced, members of the board/council should ask the staff to establish realistic evaluative tools in each of the above categories. The board/council can then help the staff refine these tools to their mutual satisfaction.
2. ESTABLISH AN ANNUAL CYCLE. It is unrealistic to expect the staff to give detailed written reports on all aspects of the work several times each year. It is also foolhardy to expect board/council members to have time to digest comprehensive reports on the entire movement at any one meeting. As a movement grows, it may even be adequate to have an in-depth look at certain aspects of the work every second or third year. Choose a logical sequence that will be acceptable to both board/council and staff.
3. LEARN FROM YOUR MISTAKES. As you go over reports and evaluate each aspect of the work, not only evaluate the work itself and generate constructive change, but interact with the staff in formulating improvements in the report's content and format.
4. AFFIRM THE POSITIVE. Use the evaluation process to affirm both the work and the workers. In the academic world too many of us find it natural to be critical, but we often forget to affirm one another. Make the experience a positive one by verbally commending the staff for all successful ventures. And if the report itself is well done, don't hesitate to tell the staff how much you appreciate the

fine way such a report is presented. One staff team I know of was greatly encouraged by a board/council member's comment that their report would be commended in any board room in the country.

5. USE WORKING COMMITTEES. As a movement grows, it is difficult for board/council members to grasp the entire spectrum of a movement. By dividing responsibilities for various aspects of the work, several board/council members will be able to gain an in-depth understanding of one aspect of the work. When a particular matter is being evaluated, committee members who have previously reviewed a report, for example, will be able to enhance the understanding of both the staff and board/council members.

15
REVIEWING PEOPLE

Guidelines for Reviewing Performance of Staff and Employees
OVERVIEW

People in any organization deserve an opportunity at regular intervals to talk about how they are doing. This is particularly important in relationships between supervisor and supervisee. As people work together for several months, their attention is naturally focused on their work. But even though they interact regularly, they may rarely, if ever, talk about how the supervisor views the worker's performance.

Supervisors and itinerant student workers who see one another infrequently have even greater difficulty in finding time to review performance. Those few occasions when they are together are often group settings for conferences, committees, or joint ministry. An opportunity for person-to-person review never occurs without prior planning.

Ideally, the organization should expect all employees to regularly evaluate and review their work in a well-rounded way. This would include a careful look at their
work loads,
job satisfaction,
performance levels,
people relationships, and
overall attitude.
Inadequate review hinders working relationships. If a supervisee suspects that his boss questions his performance, he will most likely interpret casual remarks negatively, even

though the supervisor has a positive outlook toward him. On the other hand, if a supervisee is oblivious to the supervisor's questions about his performance, he may blissfully continue his work below standards expected by his superior--and soon find himself out of a job.

THE FORCED REVIEW   Sometimes a crisis develops when either supervisor or supervisee finally says what he has been thinking. Usually the context is negative--someone has failed or missed expectations of the other party. Emotions are high, anger drives the remarks to exaggerated levels, and relationships become frayed. In the aftermath the two parties try to have a more rational review, focusing primarily on clearing up the relationship. This type of review is necessary and wise at that point, but it rarely touches on those factors that contribute the most to a wholesome and effective working relationship.

PLANNING REVIEWS   A good way to avoid these problems is to schedule reviews routinely, whether or not a problem exists.

WITH WHOM? The supervisor and supervisee, at every level in the organization.

HOW OFTEN?   The interval chosen should suit each person and situation. In clerical or manual positions, a weekly cycle may gradually become monthly or quarterly. When a field worker is first hired or moves into a new job, a review session may be wisely scheduled at monthly intervals. After the first few months, it is often adequate to schedule reviews at six-month intervals.

WHAT DO WE AIM FOR? A review primarily aims to give both supervisor and employee the chance to focus on how they are doing:

  in their work,
     in relating to one another,
        in the way they identify with the long term
        objectives of the organization.

Both should leave the interview with a sense that they have been heard, understood, respected, and affirmed.

This does not necessarily mean there will always be total agreement, and it surely does not mean affirmation for weakness or failure. But the aim is to leave the review with a positive outlook and fresh motivation to work effectively and harmoniously.

Reviews should not loom ominously in the mind of either party. If normal supervisory work is adequately carried out, the review can be a mutually uplifting time for both parties. It is unwise and damaging to relationships and the work to expect the review session to handle corrective or disciplinary matters that need to be handled promptly. When continuous wholesome supervision characterizes a relationship, the review will contain few shocking surprises.

Who Reviews the General Secretary?

In many movements no one realizes that the General Secretary himself needs the benefit of a regular review. When the Lord is prospering the work, it is easy to assume that a review of the General Secretary is superfluous. It is also easy to assume that when the board/council has received the regular reports of the General Secretary and staff, they have fulfilled their responsibilities. Not necessarily so! The effectiveness of the work of the General Secretary and his own outlook toward the work and his working relationship with the board/council need to be reviewed at least twice each year. Customarily this will be the task of the board/council chairman, or one or two members of the personnel committee of the board/council. This review should also be scheduled routinely, without respect to the apparent need for such interaction.

A further resource for a review of the General Secretary is the IFES regional secretary. He will be able to provide a broader, impartial perspective. His experience in working with other movements will be a source of creative ideas for reviewing the work.   It may even be feasible in some instances for the board/council chairman to invite the IFES regional secretary to handle one of the two reviews each year.   That way the General Secretary would have the benefit of an annual review by the board/council chairman or personnel committee AND an annual review with the IFES regional secretary.   In this arrangement, it would be important for the IFES regional secretary to give a report of the interview to the board/council chairman, with a copy to the General Secretary.   It should be understood that management decisions are not made in the review.   They might, however, flow from the review as the board/council chairman or personnel committee respond to the report of the review with the IFES regional secretary.

It is imperative that each movement choose a format and approach that harmonize with the culture and maturity of all parties concerned.

WHAT DO WE TALK ABOUT?   A prescribed agenda can insure that important topics are covered.   It can also insure that the review is interactive, rather than simply a formal lecture by the supervisor.   Among other things, a good supervisor is interested in

a. how his team members evaluate their working relationship,

b. what their aspirations may be,

c. suggestions they may have for improving their work and working environment, and

d. how the employee feels about progress being made in fulfilling the annual plan or longer-range objectives.

Guidelines

If a few basic rules are established in an organization, the review process will be much smoother and more effective. A procedure recommended for the entire organization gives everyone a sense of fairness and removes the threat of reviews conducted at the whim of the supervisor or under the pressure of a crisis.

Review Ratings

Some organizations include a rating system alongside various criteria used during the review. By assigning values to ratings, employees who perform above average may be given financial rewards as an incentive to maintain high performance. Danger: This will only be effective as supervisors are given careful guidelines so the ratings are consistent throughout the organization. Some supervisors tend to rate everyone higher; others lower. One of the top leaders needs to compare all of the ratings so they are consistent in all departments. Otherwise what is intended as a positive incentive to good work can have a negative effect on morale if employees sense unfairness.

Where ratings affect salary levels, reviews are held shortly before scheduled salary adjustments.

A Sampling of Questions

Review forms generally use a question format to guide the interview. As a team uses and adapts a format, they will find it increasingly useful. But for the first attempts, it is wise for one team or individual to draft the initial format and then introduce it to the leadership team. Though some leaders may initially balk at the idea of reviews, if their own review with their supervisor goes well, they will probably be happier to use it with their supervisees. Lesson: Begin reviews with the senior staff first.

Here are some samples of successful review questions:
SIX MONTH REVIEW (shorter than annual)
1. Review of job/position description:
     Is it up-to-date?

Are you comfortable in this job?

What do your supervisees think about your job fit? (if known)

Do you see any adjustments coming up in the next 6-12 months?

As supervisor, I wonder whether. . .

2. How are you doing personally? Anything you'd like to share about
   * family?
   * health?
   * finances?
   * peer relationships?
   * spiritual life?

3. How are the people on your team doing?
   * any special problems?
   * any change in organizational policies or procedures that would help them?
   * are they working well as a team?

4. What advice/counsel/questions do you have for me as your supervisor?
   * working relationship
   * Am I available?
   * Am I restricting you in any way you think unhelpful?
   * How can I help you more?

5. Your work.
   * Are you meeting your 6-month goals?
   * In light of this, what projections do you have for the next 6 months,
   * Have you identified any training needs?

6. Our work.
   At this 6-month point,
   * Do you see anything we should do as a team to improve our performance?
   * Do you have a concern for some other aspect of our movement that I should know about?

7. Appreciation.
   As your supervisor, I'm grateful. . .
   I look forward to. . .

ANNUAL REVIEW - A FEW SAMPLE QUESTIONS
1. List your duties.
   a. Are there some duties you are unclear about? Which?
   b. Do you dislike some duties? Which? Why?
   c. Put a % next to each duty on your list indicating the proportion of your time spent on each (total 100% only!). Are you satisfied with these percentages?
   d. What duty do you most enjoy?
   e. What do you consider the most significant thing you're doing?
2. Have your relationships been healthy, strong, weak with:

   * students   * fellow staff
   * student leaders   * supervisory staff
   * sponsors   * local committees
   * teachers/faculty   * your family

   What are some ways to improve?
3. Are you involved in a local church? Are you satisfied with this involvement? If not, what can you do about this?
4. Are you able to pace yourself? Do you think ahead and plan your week, day by day? Are you missing appointments? Did you take a day off each week?

   Contact older neighboring movements for samples of complete forms they are using.

A FEW SIMPLE RULES
1. ESTABLISH a standard review procedure for each level of the organization. Hourly employees will customarily need a different format than long-term salaried people, though the frequency should probably be the same.

2. EXPLAIN AND DISCUSS the forms and procedure with all supervisors who will be using the forms.

3. PUBLISH the review procedure throughout the organization, and explain it to each new employee.

4. DISTRIBUTE the review forms to supervisors at least one month before a scheduled deadline by which they must be completed.

5. SET APPOINTMENTS for review interviews at least a week in advance whenever possible.

6. GIVE a blank copy of the review form to each employee a few days before the review is scheduled, so they will have an opportunity to think about their own contribution to the review. [Some organizations recommend that in advance both supervisor and supervisee complete the form, rate the performance of the employee, and then during the interview compare their responses item by item.]

7. LOOK OVER and TAKE TO THE INTERVIEW the review form you used during the previous review.

8. ALLOW at least 30 minutes for each interview. Create as comfortable a climate as possible. Supervisors: Don't protect yourselves with a big desk between you and the supervisee. Consider yourself the servant of the employee to help improve his work and working relationships, and demonstrate this by giving him your undivided attention throughout the review.

9. LISTEN to each other courteously. Gently PROBE for further information.

10. SPEAK HONESTLY about improvements either of you needs to make and write them down for future reference. To avoid misunderstanding, it may be wise to read aloud what you have written. This serves, then, both as a basis for supervisory action and as a reminder of what to discuss at the next review.

11. ENCOURAGE AND COMPLIMENT the employee as much as you honestly can, so the interview ends with a

positive tone. Don't hesitate to write down these compli-
mentary aspects as well.

12. DON'T HESITATE TO PRAY together before, during
and/or after the review.

13. FOLLOW THROUGH on any action you have agreed
to take.

14. KEEP CONFIDENCES secure when the employee has
requested confidentiality.

16
TEAMWORK

Teamwork is an essential foundation principle in our movements, since our purposes cannot be fulfilled without a large group of people being involved. We cannot possibly, nor would we wish to, hire people to do all of the work involved in evangelizing, discipling and equipping students.

1. Our purposes lead us immediately into a group or team experience:

a. In the schools: If somehow we found a large amount of money so that we could hire people to work full time with every group of 50 or more students, each worker would soon be training students to lead Bible studies, to witness to their friends, and to learn to disciple the new converts. What began as a tidy group of people on a payroll would quickly become a mix of volunteers, inquirers into the faith, and paid workers.

b. In the staff: Once we have more than one paid staff person, we begin an elemental team. Furthermore, even one staff person is immediately a part of a team which hired him, a team which supports him financially, and a team which prays for him.

2. Several essentials to Christian growth demand that we think "teamwork" in many aspects of our student movements:

a. We need the gifts of other members of the Body of Christ in order to grow. I Corinthians 12 makes this very clear, as in verse 7 Paul writes "Now to each one the manifestation of the Spirit is given for the common good."

The entire chapter expands this idea to help us understand that as believers we must relate to one another, benefiting from the various gifts God has given our fellow members, and expressing our own gifts for their benefit.

b. I recall that years ago Stacey Woods, our founding IFES General Secretary, spoke often of the "priesthood of all believers." He emphasized that the Bible teaches that each person who enters God's family becomes a link between men and God: one who can assist people in entering God's kingdom and also one who can express God's love and justice in the world so that His will may be done on earth as it is in heaven. Those of us who were fortunate enough to know Stacey personally know how much this attitude helped us become more responsible and active Christians in our universities. We recognized immediately that we were a vital part of God's team, not just passive spectators at meetings. Our prayers at the 7:25 a.m. prayer meeting were making a difference in the lives of our friends for whom we prayed. Probably no other single factor stimulated spiritual vitality more than this sense of our being co-workers with God.

Every Christian (including the student who has just become a Christian) is a member of God's team, and deserves to be included in our team plans. True, he may have a lot to learn, but how better to learn than as a working member of the group? As the Apostle Paul wrote to Timothy:

"And the things you have heard me say in the presence of many witnesses entrust to reliable men who will also be qualified to teach others." (2 Timothy 2:2)

This is how our basic purpose is fulfilled: people influencing others to believe in Jesus Christ and to follow him, not because they're paid to do so, but because they have become new creatures in Christ.

Some Practical Observations
- Working with a team can be more enjoyable than working alone.
- Working with others sharpens my own motivation to do well, as I see others creatively using their gifts.
- Many tasks call for skills I may not possess. Others may excel in them.
- Some jobs I don't like to do, but another person loves to do them. Why not give them the joy of doing something they like?!
- Even the Lord called twelve to be with him, and later sent out the disciples two by two.
- One of life's greatest joys is to see a miscellaneous collection of people develop into an effective working team.

A General Secretary is in a unique position to set the pace for the entire movement as he enlists the help of graduates, students, faculty, volunteers, prayer warriors.

I Chronicles 28:21 quotes David's marvelous assurance to Solomon: "and every willing man skilled in any craft will help you in all the work." This short section at the end of I Chronicles 28 merits study. I have often claimed this promise for the student work, reasoning with the Lord that if He made this provision for the earthly temple, how much more will He not want to do so for the heavenly temple being built in students on campus.

Activities of a Team Leader
planning	organizing, policy-making
enlisting people	training
pastoring	coordinating
reviewing	

defining jobs, delegating work, supervising

Steps in Team Building
1. IN THE BEGINNING . . .

Each General Secretary finds himself a part of a team which may be small or large, depending upon the nation he works in. Customarily this team has already defined its purposes. Let us assume that before he accepts this assignment he has understood and committed himself to the purposes of the movement. If the purpose is not clear, all of the suggestions which follow will be difficult, if not impossible to implement.

An initial task of the new leader is to discover the answer to the question "What have I got myself into?"

■ Who is on the team that I've inherited (paid staff, volunteers)?

■ What are their hopes, aspirations, skills, problems, jobs?

■ How do they relate to one another?

■ What do they expect of me as General Secretary? . . . and how do their expectations harmonize with those (if any) expressed by those who hired me?

■ Do these expectations harmonize with the purposes of the movement? With what I believe is God's vision?

■ What resources do we have?

■ What facilities are already available (campsites, offices, equipment)?

■ How about finances? Are budgets used? Are they met?

■ What means are used in funding the movement?

■ What ministries, if any, are already underway?

2. GATHERING A TEAM

Only after assessing the situation you've inherited will it be feasible to lay plans for building your team. If the people God has already brought into the movement are effectively working toward the purposes, you will find them a valuable resource for the future. Very likely they

will also be your most effective means of discovering future
team members, since they are already in touch with people
who are involved in the ministry. One profitable element
in each meeting with your team (whether it's only two or
a dozen) is to talk about:

   a) The kind of people needed for the team; (What gifts,
   skills should they possess?)
   b) The people we are now in touch with who have these
   gifts; (Deeds done are the best indicators of gifts.)
   c) What kinds of experience can we encourage them to
   gain? (student training camps, visiting a neighboring
   campus with a staff person, becoming part of a staff
   team for a campus mission, reading THE DAY OF HIS
   POWER, etc.)

Then after the discussion, prayer for each person by name
and for the need of team workers is extremely important.

   Then Jesus said to his disciples, `The harvest is plentiful
but the workers are few. Ask the Lord of the harvest,
therefore, to send out workers into his harvest field.'
(Matthew 9:37, 38.)

Student work demands the highest calibre of person who
will often have many other calls beckoning; only the Lord
of the Harvest will be able to call them into the movement,
whether as part-time volunteers or full-time workers.

A SAMPLE TEAM MEETING AGENDA
   Introduction of new people
   Brief overview of agenda
   Ask for entries to agenda from group members
   Prayer - not rushed, nor left to the end
   Main topic/presentation plus discussion
   Prayer re main topic
   Break
   Miscellaneous business items
   10-minute spotlight for each team member, with prayer

Coming events, next meeting's agenda, date, place
Concluding prayer
Celebration, social time, etc.

3. BUILDING A TEAM; DEVELOPING OWNERSHIP

Even as the human body has complex interrelationships, so the variety among team members makes leadership a challenging task. But the bonus for us as Christian leaders is the presence of the Holy Spirit among us. He not only enables the leader, but also indwells each member of the team. If I as a leader live with this awareness, it enables me to expect more of each team member and this helps them grow accordingly. I remember when as a student my staff member urged me to speak to a church congregation--my first preaching opportunity. Without the staff person's encouragement, I would never have dared. Her confidence in the Holy Spirit in me helped her to pray boldly for me and to urge me on my way in Christian ministry.

Another quality that enhances team building is genuine love. If I as a team leader love my team members, the entire group will be encouraged to live in love with one another. This doesn't mean that I must _like_ everything about each person, but it does mean that I care deeply about them, appreciate them, and let them know that I do so.

Team building among university people is best accomplished by a collegial (participatory) leadership style. Involvement in planning, deciding, and implementing ministry objectives will build team unity and energy. Lack of involvement will lead to restlessness, lack of motivation, and private agendas of various kinds. If I as a leader have a new idea, suggest and explain it to the team, and yet fail to win their support for the idea, it is wise to listen to their objections, lead them in revising (or discarding!) the idea, and then implement the united revision. If the team I have gathered is a high quality team, it should not be surprising nor embarrassing to listen to improvements and changes they suggest!

Incidentally, customarily before hiring people for leadership roles, I have told them that I am not hiring them to agree with me, but to express their best judgments. Their contribution to our ministry will only be at its best if they speak their genuine opinions freely. Then arguments pro and con can help refine and improve the decision, making it much easier for each member of the team to support the decision as it is implemented.

Team building is enhanced as the leader converses privately between sessions with various members of the team. The leader may sense one member's reluctance to speak on a certain issue and quietly ask that person what he thinks about the matter. Or in team meeting someone may have spoken in vigorous opposition to an issue which the team accepted. A private conversation later can help assuage restless emotions and reinforce acceptance of the person despite the difference of opinion. This kind of pastoral role is often one of the most rewarding ministries of leadership.

4. NURTURE AND DISCIPLINE

A team will mature and flourish only with careful nurture. Some of the factors which encourage growth include:

* Bible study together
* Prayer as a group: adoration, confession, thanksgiving, supplication (ACTS)
* Worship
* Readiness to affirm one another
* Openness to rebuke, correction from one another
* Occasional discussions about how team members are functioning together
* Having fun together
* Celebrating together after a successful event.

Note: The SMALL GROUP LEADERS HANDBOOK published by US IVP has many good ideas which may work in your culture as well.

Discipline in the team is often ticklish, partly because it is difficult to determine what is causing a problem, and partly because a strong team encourages differences of opinion rather than uniformity. Unity, yes. Uniformity, no. The leader must be very sensitive in drawing the fine distinction between constructive and harmful differences.

It is clear that if immoral or unethical issues are involved, the leader must take action without delay. But where unity is threatened by a difference of opinion, the action required may vary from a private talk with a single individual, to an open dialogue among team members.

One of the most difficult problems in student work is confirming reports which indicate a staff person needs discipline. A simple guideline is to insist upon two or three witnesses before taking action, as Paul says in I Timothy 5:19: "Do not entertain an accusation against an elder unless it is brought by two or three witnesses."

5. REVIEW

One of the finest tools available to a leader is the review. It gives a natural opportunity to confirm and affirm good performance, to assess the way in which team members evaluate performance, to discern how they feel about their work, and to agree on steps for improvement.

When should we review? From one vantage point, we review each time we report on an event or task, and then again when we lay plans for the next event. As the team talks over what they have been doing, they naturally evaluate the effectiveness of their work and make suggestions for improvement. This is an ideal climate in which to affirm good performance and to lovingly encourage improvement.

Furthermore, a team meeting enables any member of the team to assume a role of encourager or evaluator, thus lightening the task of the team leader. I recall various evaluation sessions after weekend conferences when our staff perspectives were corrected by the helpful comments of our colleagues who had talked with students who expressed particular appreciation for a Bible study group or book review that the leader had felt was less effective than he wished.

Another aspect of review is a regularly scheduled review cycle at six-monthly intervals when each individual worker has an opportunity to sit down with his team leader and talk over any or every aspect of the work. This is usually most easily done if a standard review format is worked out by the team members in advance or prepared by the team leader. Many things that may be overlooked in the normal supervisory schedule may naturally be considered in a six-monthly review. Problems can often be unearthed at an early stage, rather than waiting for them to reach a boiling point. Furthermore, affirmation and encouragement flow naturally during such a review session. Samples of review forms may be available through your IFES regional secretary.

17
VOLUNTEERS

IFES is a fellowship of national evangelical unions each of which aims to be indigenous: self-governing, self-propagating, and self-supporting.

Since most nations do not have the resources to support a large team of paid workers, an indigenous work is only possible through the combined efforts of VOLUNTEERS--people whom God uses in evangelism, discipleship, mission outreach, and in every aspect of an indigenous work: governing, propagating, and supporting. If every worker were salaried, the drain on the resources of the Christian community and the time and effort devoted to fund raising would be staggering.

Fortunately, our student unions serve as an ideal training ground for ministry, since student volunteers evangelize, serve on the local executive, lead Bible studies and prayer groups, and carry out all functions of the student union. Their voluntary service as students prepares them to serve the Church (including the student movement) for the rest of their lives.

How can we more effectively harness the time and talents available within our own nation by using volunteers at other levels in our movement--people who choose to use some of their free time to serve with us in establishing and extending our ministry to students?

It may appear that everyone is already busy and over-committed. But in what activities? How about those Christians who are not yet involved in ministry with the student movement? Even in nations with a small Christian population, it is not unusual to find talented people with positive potential for student ministry. How can we harness this potential?

In this chapter we'll be exploring ways in which we can recruit and supervise volunteers so they can enable us to accomplish ministry goals which would otherwise be assigned to salaried staff.

What is a Volunteer?

A dictionary defines a volunteer as "one who performs a service of his own free will", or "one who voluntarily offers himself for a service or undertaking." In IFES, volunteers do not earn a salary or wage for their services.

What Makes a Person Want to Volunteer His Services for a Particular Cause?

1. A person must have a READINESS TO ASSIST others and find satisfaction in being of service. In this we are fortunate in having the superb example of our Master, who said, "whoever wants to become great among you must be your servant, and whoever wants to be first must be slave of all. For even the Son of Man did not come to be served, but to serve, and to give his life as a ransom for many." (Mark 10:43-45) He expects this kind of spirit to character-ize His followers. And so we can expect those who are discipled in our movements, and other Christians, to possess this spirit of service.

2. A person will volunteer to help a ministry or project which he thinks is WORTHWHILE. Among competing interests, he considers this ministry valuable and important. If God blesses his ministry and supervisors and colleagues affirm him, he will want to continue to assist for many years.

3. Potential volunteers will choose your organization if they KNOW AND RESPECT people in the movement.

Prerequisites for Volunteer Involvement

1. A WILLINGNESS to serve.
2. The TIME available when the service is needed.
3. The CHRISTIAN FAITH AND CHARACTER which are required to perform the service. Those in direct student ministry must be able to sign the Basis of Faith, live an exemplary Christian life, and demonstrate an understanding of and commitment to the purposes of the national movement.
4. The SKILLS, or potential skills, to perform the service needed.
5. The COMMITMENT to fulfill a particular ministry that the leadership of the movement defines.
6. A CONTRACT TO PERFORM A PARTICULAR SERVICE from an authorized person in the national movement. This represents a commitment from the movement to the volunteer, and formalizes the volunteer's commitment (as in 5, above). This may be verbal, though written contracts which include goals and job descriptions are recommended.

What is the Best Way to Recruit Volunteers?

Although the word "volunteers" conveys the idea of people coming forward and offering to be of help, the best way of recruiting qualified volunteers is by personal invitation. Why? Because most highly qualified people are already busy in other activities and haven't thought of helping the student movement. And even those qualified may not consider themselves adequate for the task without the reassurance that a definite invitation gives.

Screening Volunteers

Volunteers need to be screened almost as carefully as full-time staff. If they are entrusted with ministry to students, they should be of the same calibre as full-time staff. From the vantage point of the student, the volunteer may be the only official representative of the organization whom they regularly see. The unseen difference is simply their source of income and the amount of time they devote to student ministry.

It is wise to make fairly careful inquiries about prospective volunteers before inviting them to assist you. It may be awkward for you and devastating to the prospect if you back down after having made the invitation. Try to get three (never less than two) confirming references before making a firm invitation. Another way of approaching prospects is to invite them to APPLY for a volunteer position. But with senior people this lends an air of uncertainty that may seem disrespectful to them.

Use a WRITTEN APPLICATION FORM as a basis for screening prospects. Such a form should contain 1) all of the basic factual data (name, address, phone, church, experience in the student movement, education, etc.); 2) name, address, and phone of at least three people who will vouch for the suitability of the candidate; and 3) a section for listing their time and ministry preferences.

Promptly THANK applicants for their applications, and at the same time give them some indication of HOW LONG it may be before they hear from you again. A letter, postal card, or telephone call will help put them at ease as they wait.

If the screening process is prolonged, some kind of contact with them each month helps keep their interest and expectations alive. Otherwise they may lose interest and be unavailable when you finally make your decision.

Don't Forget the Local Team

Once the applicant is approved for service with the movement, it is wise (if the assignment is to a work already established) to let the local team give their approval of the person AND work through the assignment the person will have. [In many cases, the local team will make the initial contact and be ready to welcome the volunteer as soon as the national movement confirms approval.]

Contract (Agreement)

The CONTRACT between the movement and the volunteer may be very similar to that used for full-time employees, except for the financial aspect. Such a contract should clearly state:

1. the title and nature of the job to be done (job description);
2. the person to whom the volunteer is responsible (reports to:);
3. the length of time the contract covers;
4. any special conditions, such as reimbursement of expenses, training sessions which are expected, central staff conferences or events, etc.
5. signature with date for both the volunteer and the movement's representative.

If this contract has been reviewed by both the local team and the central staff, the new volunteer should find a secure and welcome climate from the very first day at work.

A face-to-face INTERVIEW with the applicant is the best way of confirming the appointment and going over the contract. At this interview the representative of the movement should give the applicant ample opportunity to ask questions and be ready to negotiate modifications. Serious changes must, of course, be taken back to the local team before the contract is finalized. This may seem a bothersome step, but is a vital one if the volunteer is to have a positive experience from the very beginning. Careful advance work of this sort pays dividends in overall morale in the organization. It shows respect both for the local team and for the new worker.

Introducing the Volunteer to His Job

Once the contract is clear, it is best to accompany the volunteer on his first visit to a student group or conference. In some nations geographic limitations may make this impossible. In this case it may be feasible for the volunteer to assist in an intercollegiate conference where he/she can be introduced to the students they will be working with.

Even when distance forbids such an introduction, it is wise to have some kind of supervisory contact with the volunteer every week for the first month, and then at least once each month for the first year. This will give the worker an opportunity to receive direction, confirmation of work accomplished, and encouragement. In an ideal arrangement, the new person works alongside an experienced worker for the first few weeks or months, and thus is able to be taught by demonstration and immediate evaluation of his work.

Volunteers for Projects or Office Tasks

When a person has volunteered to assist with routine tasks, working alongside an experienced person, most of the above requirements may be waived. Only their willingness and skills may need to be determined in advance, since they always have someone at hand to give direction.

Volunteers who assist at conferences in small group leadership or administrative support will almost always be involved at the local level where most of the screening procedures have already been handled spontaneously. Thus the careful procedures outlined above are not needed.

How Can we Help People Choose Our Movement as a Place of Voluntary Service?

1. By DEMONSTRATING that we ourselves are enthusiastically involved in student ministry, whether we are on staff or board/council.

2. By TELLING graduates, friends, and people in churches what God is doing in and through our student movement. This will include both word-of-mouth and print, audio and/or visual materials. Student teams who go to minister in communities will be natural communicators of what God is doing.

3. By listing and freely telling about OPENINGS we have for ministry at the local, regional and national levels.

4. By INVITING potentially qualified individuals to participate in our conferences, on-campus evangelistic events, staff training days, or local graduates fellowship gatherings. First-hand experience is an ideal way to whet the appetites of potential volunteers.

5. By PRESENTING TO GRADUATING SENIORS the challenge of ministry in the movement.

6. By INVITING STUDENTS from one campus to minister with staff people on nearby campuses. In this way they get a taste of the kind of ministry a non-residential person would have if serving as a volunteer.

7. By PRAYING specifically for individuals whom you observe have the qualifications for ministry as a volunteer, asking God to give them a call and prosper your contacts with them. If you work with a team, prayer for these people should be a regular part of your team meeting.

8. By having a SPECIAL EVENT when people who would like to consider volunteering for ministry may have a chance to meet staff and board/council people. Formal presentations showing the nature and extent of the ministry coupled with time for questions and discussion have proved effective ways of enlisting volunteers.

9. By offering TRAINING COURSES for volunteers which will equip them to serve not only among students but wherever God may later call them to minister.

How to Affirm Volunteers

1. Establish CLEAR GOALS for their work so you can commend them when they are accomplished.

2. Have regular SUPERVISORY CONTACT so you can affirm their good work, make corrections before mistakes become entrenched, and give them a feeling that you consider their ministry valuable.

3. Get them INVOLVED IN PLANNING as soon as they have some experience. Planning time is ideal training time, since the person learns WHY as well as WHAT.

4. ACKNOWLEDGE THEIR REPORTS and respond to phone calls without delay. This also helps them feel secure and valued.

5. LISTEN to their stories, their questions and problems. When visiting them, give them (and their spouse) time with you personally, not just in ministry.

6. COMMEND them for good work in front of other volunteers and their colleagues. Sure, you run the risk of pride setting in, but you'll almost always gain far more than you lose.

7. INVITE them to staff meetings, introduce them to local board/council members, give them experiences of working with other volunteers, visit the student unions with them when you are able.

8. Have an annual APPRECIATION EVENT when each volunteer is affirmed publicly, by students, board/council and colleagues.

9. Encourage prayer warriors to PRAY for the volunteer; list names of volunteers in your prayer guide; and of course pray for them yourself.

18
GRADUATES

Immediately prior to the 1987 IFES General Committee, a group of graduates and board/council members gathered to help one another in fulfilling their ministry within student movements. During the course of the four-day consultation, the 30 participants from 25 different nations unanimously agreed and submitted a formal proposal to the IFES executive committee pointing out that 1) although a growing group of graduates are serving Christ throughout the world, 2) there is a high fall-out rate, indicating they need continuing help, and 3) many graduates lose contact with our movements. Furthermore, it was agreed that student movements are going to survive and grow only if graduates of the student work are encouraged and enabled to assist the movements that have nurtured them.

Although it will be impossible to relate all of the helpful ideas which were shared during that consultation, we will select some of the concepts which can assist general secretaries and board/council members in developing an effective ministry by and among graduates.

Some Definitions

For purposes of our discussion here, let us define graduates as "those people who have completed their academic studies and are now in the workplace." For those movements with secondary school work, this may on occasion mean high school graduates. Customarily, however, we will think of university/college graduates.

In our discussion we will also use the term "volunteer." A volunteer is a person who ministers without remunera-

tion, even though h/she may be personally invited and
urged to participate.

Why are Graduates Important to Our IFES Movements?
1. They UNDERSTAND the movement because of personal
involvement. They know it from the inside, from first-hand
experience.
2. They APPRECIATE and VALUE the movement because
they have personally benefitted from the ministry of the
movement while an undergraduate or graduate student.
3. They KNOW PEOPLE who are still involved with the
movement. Recent graduates will know Christian students
who are yet in the student group, staff, Christian profes-
sors, and recent alumni who either were graduated with
them or a year or two before them. In many cases they
will also be praying for some non-Christian friends who
have not yet been graduated.
4. They have varying amounts of DISCRETIONARY TIME
in which to assist the movement according to their ability
and willingness.
5. They posses some SKILLS which are needed by the
movement. Among the skills will be not only their primary
field of training, but also those skills they developed while
members of the student group--Bible study leadership,
evangelistic outreach, answering questions of science and
faith, organizing events, praying for people in need, etc.
6. They live, work, and go to church in COMMUNITY with
people who are potentially able to assist the movement.
Their friendship can serve as a natural bridge to people
who would have no other means of learning about the
movement.
7. They are very likely WAGE EARNERS who have a desire
to give a portion of their income to Christian ministry.
Surely some of their giving should be earmarked for the

movement which ministered to them while they were students.

Is Depending upon Graduates a Sign of Weakness in the Movement?

While most of us may readily admit that the student movement needs graduates, we may feel apologetic about asking graduates to assist. They are busy at work; they are beginning to take leadership in their local church and are in demand for committee work and teaching church school classes; they may be recently married and have family obligations; they have just set up a new home and are busy getting settled; they may be taking night courses for graduate degrees, etc.

If one looked at their involvement as students, a similar list of demands would emerge: studies, exams, term papers, labs, time with parents, part-time jobs, etc. Every stage of life offers a long list of obligations.

But even as students active in our movements decided that Christian ministry was important, so our graduates must MAKE CHOICES if they are to engage in Christian ministry. Is the student work important in God's economy? Is presenting the Gospel of Christ to the students of THIS GENERATION a part of God's plan? Is teaching students to study God's Word worth the effort required? Was the impact of the movement in our own lives worth the effort our staff and leaders invested?

It is the privilege and responsibility of the board/council and General Secretary to a) face these questions squarely, and b) assist the graduates in finding God's will for the part they should have in student ministry. Without leadership from the General Secretary and board/council, it is unlikely that the movement will find enough gifted graduates to do the work.

If insufficient graduates are recruited as non-paid workers, the movement will be forced to consider increasing the size of the paid staff, with all of its attendant financial and administrative pressures. It is good to remember that historically God has used people who received no financial remuneration to establish and lead student groups. It is also true that some of the world's fastest-growing churches (China) have developed with few or no paid workers.

The development and growth of student groups has also been nurtured by those faculty and graduates who have given freely and voluntarily of their talents in leading, counseling, organizing intercollegiate events, providing hospitality and transportation, and countless other services to students.

Is it too much to expect that God will continue to call out volunteers to help build His Church in the lives of students? A resounding answer to that question is readily available in Africa. It has been surprising to learn that our largest IFES movement, NIFES (Nigeria), has had over 30,000 student participants with a paid staff of fewer than ten! Surely a small army of volunteers must be providing the basic support required to develop a movement of that magnitude.

If God can do that in Nigeria, can He not call volunteers in many other nations? Graduate involvement is a sign of strength, not weakness! "Ask the Lord of the harvest, therefore, to send out workers into his harvest field." (Matthew 9:38)

Some Ways to Enlist Graduate Helpers
A SIMPLE SOLUTION:
1. Discover what tasks are suitable for graduates in your movement.
2. Learn what talents your graduates have.

3. Work out ways of putting 1 and 2 together. That simple solution can be a very demanding task in a large movement, but even in a small movement there are many factors that make the process difficult.

Some of the Problems that are encountered most frequently include:

Lack of vision of graduates' potential on the part of the leadership team. (General Secretary, senior staff and board/council)

Lack of commitment to the movement by the graduates themselves.

Lack of orientation and training programs for graduate volunteers.

Lack of specific task assignments for those who volunteer.

Lack of appreciation shown to those who participate, often at great personal cost.

An Effective Program for Graduates can be developed if the leadership team:

1. Studies the feasibility of having a more definite ministry by graduates throughout the movement and makes a deliberate decision to ask a task force to recommend a plan of action. (This should include specific ministries for graduates, ways of recruiting participants, allocating resources such as time and money so it can be done.)

2. Reviews the recommended plan and then makes a commitment to implement it with resource allocation (people and money) over a prescribed time period.

3. Reviews progress at various checkpoints along the way to insure that the plan is workable and being implemented.

Three Things to Keep in Mind

1. The best time to train graduates is while they are still undergraduates.

2. The best time to suggest that graduates participate is while they are undergraduates.

3. The best time to tie down a specific assignment for a graduate is before he/she graduates. [When employment requires a change of location, a name, address and phone number of a leader in the new location will help the graduate stay in touch with the movement.]

Kinds of Tasks Graduates Have Successfully Performed:
In the School/On Campus
   * Leading Bible discussions in student living units.
   * Leading evangelistic discussions in student living units or elsewhere on campus.
   * Counseling students about personal problems.
   * Tutoring students in academic subjects.
   * Meeting with student exec or small group leader as a resource person.
   * Meeting privately with the student president between exec meetings for prayer and counsel.
   * Helping resolve problems between individuals in a student group.
   * Participating in prayer groups with students.
   * Praying for/with individual students.
   * Assisting students in finding employment.

Off Campus
   * Hospitality for individual students and for student exec meetings, group social events, visiting Christian students
   * A home away from home for exhausted, homesick, or lonely students.
   * Assistance with transportation to conferences.

* Planning menus, buying food, cooking for conferences, lining up suitable conference sites, handling arrangements with camp manager, etc.
* Serving as cabin leaders, small group leaders, speakers, or recreation coordinators at intercollegiate events.
* Convening, hosting prayer meetings to intercede for the student ministry.
* Ordering books, managing booktables, supplying books to student groups or intercollegiate events.

Nationally
* Serving as regional or area director.
* Serving as board/council or committee member.
* Contributing money to the movement.
* Representing the movement to church denominational gatherings.
* Representing the movement as a member of a para-church board.
* Advising the General Secretary or board/council in matters of special expertise, e.g. finance, law, business management, theology.
* Informing people in the secular and Christian communities about the movement and its ministries and needs.
* Helping the movement understand the implications of changes in the world of their professional interest, particularly if they are faculty members or leaders in government.

How Do We Put All of This Together?
As we've already pointed out, the first step lies with the leadership ministry team. They must decide to give priority to graduates' ministry. The General Secretary along with the board/council must make the decision and then enlist the entire organization in implementing the vision. It

cannot be done by simply hiring one individual to "develop graduates work."

Step One may well be scheduling a 30- to 60-minute brainstorm at the next joint gathering of staff and board/council. Basic questions such as the following would be useful starting points in most cases:

1. Why are graduates important to the future of our movement?

2. In what ways are graduates serving our movement now?

3. What kinds of tasks could graduates perform in our movement?

4. What are we doing now to harness the graduates who are already in the workplace?

5. What are we now doing to prepare students for their role as graduates?

6. Who should be on a task force to develop a workable plan for our consideration? (Don't forget to include a couple of graduates!)

7. When should they report back to us?

8. How can we harness prayer for this ministry?

Effective graduates can benefit every part of the movement, right down to the small group in a dorm on campus. A gifted graduate may be invited to a living unit to lead a training session for small group leaders, or a student may find that a graduate has volunteered to tutor him for his heavy course in calculus. He may even be able to invite his friend from another country over to the home of a graduate for a taste of Christian hospitality.

The living unit or each individual chapter will benefit from the ministry of graduates only if the ANNUAL PLANS of the leadership team include adequate entries for implementing the vision.

Some suggested entries for a movement's annual plan:
1. goals and plans for a session at spring conferences to introduce graduating seniors to the potential of ministry after graduation;
2. specific plans for training graduates in their ministries at once-per-week three-hour training sessions on Saturday afternoons during the first two months of the next term;
3. an annual cycle of training events for graduates who wish to become qualified to teach students how to lead Bible discussions;
4. entries in each full-time staff person's job description defining how he/she will relate to the ministry of graduates;
5. a session at several staff meetings to help the entire team re-think and prayerfully incorporate graduates into their work.

JUST A REMINDER: When holding a discussion like the above, use a chalkboard or easel pad to record the contributions. That will help focus everyone's attention and keep them aware of what others have suggested. During creative brainstorms, people will often be formulating their own contribution while others are talking. The notes on the board will keep them abreast of what others have suggested while they were busy concentrating on their next idea.

19
MONEY

Most student workers are people-focused, caring, and eager to help students come to know Christ as Savior and Lord. The idea that they need to pay attention to money annoys them, because it diverts energy and attention away from the students whom they love.

But without money the workers suffer, the work is restricted, and discontent festers in homes and among people in almost every part of the organization.

Some may think that the ideal setup would be to find workers who would journey like the early disciples without staff, bag, bread, money, or an extra tunic (see Luke 9:3). But would it really be better?

Isn't the act of sharing and giving one of the hallmarks of true Christianity? Sharing with those who minister the Gospel is a great privilege, and clearly taught by Paul, for example, in 2 Corinthians 8 and 9. He tells us that members of the body of Christ are bound together through giving and thanksgiving when generosity characterizes their fellowship.

Those of us who have known the hardships endured by staff (especially wives) when their already low salaries are delayed or in arrears, affirm that leaders of each movement need to insure that salaries are adequate and paid promptly.

Money will play a constructive role in every aspect of the life of a movement only when carefully established policies and procedures are adopted and followed.

In this chapter we will briefly summarize the key financial factors that each movement must resolve.

Some Basics in Finance

Movements will ordinarily be funded by freewill gifts from graduates, churches, friends, and trusts.

Gifts are given to the central office to enable the movement to fulfill the purpose for which it was established.

The Board/Council is responsible for the proper handling of funds. This includes:

* keeping a careful RECORD of each gift,
* sending a proper RECEIPT to the donor,
* PAYING BILLS on time, including salaries and necessary taxes,
* publishing a MONTHLY REPORT of the financial transactions for review by the General Secretary and board/council,
* hiring an outside AUDITOR to review the transactions of the year and confirm their accuracy, and
* publishing an ANNUAL REPORT which not only summarizes all transactions of the year, but also gives a comparison of the overall financial condition of the movement a year previously.

Government taxes for employee welfare, often called "social security", will need to be paid routinely.

Expenses incurred in the work of the staff and other employees are to be reimbursed by the movement. These ordinarily include travel, telephone, postage, meals and housing away from home, supplies, etc. Proper expense forms will make this easier.

Money for the work handed to staff should routinely be turned in to the office so a proper receipt can be sent to the original donor.

Planning

Careful planning enables a movement to temper the wild fluctuations of income and expense which accompany a casual approach to both spending money and receiving it. Without planning, funds may be depleted by unexpected bills which accompany a national conference, an unexpected slump in donations, or the purchase of a large (and needed) piece of equipment.

A financial plan is often called a budget. A dictionary definition is "an estimate, often itemized, of expected income and expense for a given period in the future."

Here are a few guidelines to assist in annual financial planning (budgeting):

1. Review your objectives for the year ahead. Enumerate all those which require money, including full-time employees (who will need both salary and benefits, such as health insurance, pension, social security, etc.);

* travel expenses;
* routine expenses such as rent, electricity, telephone, postage, printing, supplies;
* conferences which will not be self-supporting;
* campus evangelistic missions;
* and money required for bills that will need to be paid before the money comes in from registrants to conferences or for materials sent.

2. Each of these items then needs to be expressed on a schedule of payment, month by month, throughout the year. For example, January may have entries of this sort:

People
    salary
    social security
    pension
    health insurance
    income tax withholding
Travel -   employee travel

Office -   rent   printing
            electricity   supplies
            telephone   insurance
            postage   cleaning
Events -   deposit on conference site for summer
               conference
            printing & mailing folders

3. Total the expenses for the 12 months. In addition add perhaps 5- or 10% for contingencies which may arise. Otherwise if you have an unexpected repair bill on a vehicle, for example, you will need to make cuts elsewhere or make a crisis appeal for funds.

4. Make a projection of what your INCOME is likely to be during the next year.

Probable sources are donations from:

a. those who have given previously,

b. churches, friends, and relatives of new staff,

c. recent graduates who are wage earners for the first time,

d. trusts or foundations which you are approaching.

You may also have income from conference registrants, book sales, or sale of property.

Some student groups raise money for the movement through car washes or other projects which generate money. In a few nations student groups make a commitment of a certain portion of their own budget to help support the movement.

5. Now project overall income into a month-by-month schedule. Customarily income is not received evenly, but rather has peaks and valleys that are repeated each year. If you have records of monthly receipts for previous years, use that as a guide to indicate what percentage of income is likely to be received each month.

6. Compare each month's expense and income to arrive at what is sometimes known as your cash flow curve. It is unlikely that inflow and outgo will be equal.

7. This brings you to the next phase of financial planning, which is making a plan to handle payments during the months when expense exceeds income. We will devote the next section to that subject.

Controlling Cash

If your budget is carefully worked out, you will have expected certain months when income will not be adequate to cover all of the payments which must be made. How will your movement handle this?

Various options exist:

1. Delay payments to people outside the movement: your landlord, firms from whom you have bought materials and equipment, travel agents, government tax or social security agencies, etc.

2. Delay obligations within the movement, such as staff salaries, reimbursement for travel expenses.

3. Establish a line of credit at a bank to enable you to borrow the needed funds in months of shortfall.

4. Establish a stabilization fund which will be accessible when a shortage occurs.

5. Terminate workers, mortgage or sell property.

Which of the above is most desirable?

Obviously option 4 is the smoothest and least oppressive approach. By planning ahead and building a reserve year by year, the months of shortfall will be weathered most easily. Sometimes a few large donors will be willing to help establish this fund for the welfare of the people in the movement. Another approach is to build into your budget each year a specified amount which will be added to the reserve fund. Just this past week I received a letter from a non-IFES organization indicating that they had only been able to pay salaries and obligations last month because four staff people had agreed to accept delayed payment of salaries. IVCF-USA handled its cash flow this way during the first twenty years of its life. All of us old-timers remember how during the autumn we would customarily be two months behind in salary until people's generosity blossomed along with the Christmas spirit. Unfortunately a number of excellent staff found it necessary to leave the movement, since they could not properly care for their families.

This policy was changed at the time Charles Troutman returned from Australia and pointed out to our board that in reality the staff were the bankers of the organization. And they were the people least able to go without regular salaries, since the salaries of secular workers and graduates, in particular, were much higher than those of Christian workers.

Establishing a line of credit with a bank is an option which movements should consider. When the movement is very small, graduates or board/council members who have resources may need to co-sign such an arrangement. If so, it is then vitally important that the entire organization insure that the line of credit is repaid at the agreed date. This deadline provides a natural opportunity for staff, board and graduates to cooperate in both prayer and sharing the needs of the work in their circle of influence. Rarely should the expected repayment of such a line of credit exceed 12 months.

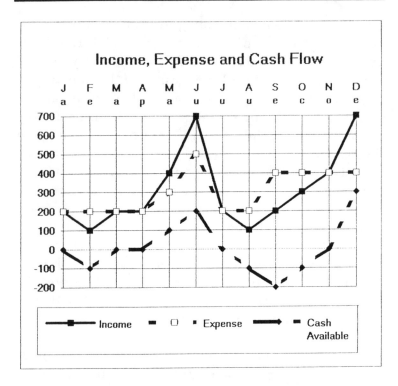

The graph above depicts the following:

	Income	Expense	Cash Available	To-Date Cash
Ja	200	200	0	0
Fe	100	200	-100	-100
Ma	200	200	0	-100
Ap	200	200	0	-100
Ma	400	300	100	0
Ju	700	500	200	200
Ju	200	200	0	200
Au	100	200	-100	100
Se	200	400	-200	-100
Oc	300	400	-100	-200
No	400	400	0	-200
De	700	400	300	100
	3700	3600		

From the graph you see that the maximum cash to be borrowed is $200 in October and November. This is 6% of annual expenses. Some movements find they need a line of credit or fund equal to two or three months' salary. Study historic patterns of income to assess your need.

Safeguards

Money, sex and power are commonly recognized as the three areas most likely to subvert people holding public office. Unfortunately, the same trio hold sway in Christian ministries. It is therefore important to insure that money is handled properly, with cross checks which will keep people from undue temptation.

Sometimes we think that our dedicated staff are immune from this temptation. Unfortunately, I know of several people within national student movements who have diverted money from the organization for their own personal use. In other cases careless accounting procedures have led to the unidentified disappearance of large sums of money. Each diversion is not only a sin by the individual, but a great risk to the reputation of the entire Church of Jesus Christ.

A few years ago a group of Christian leaders in the United States established a code of responsible stewardship in order to prevent a) financial abuses, and b) a threat of intervention by the government to correct improprieties. They named their agency The Evangelical Council for Financial Accountability, which now has several hundred member organizations, including IVCF-USA. All members pledge to abide by the code, which should be useful in any nation. It is reproduced below.

"Seven Standards of Responsible Stewardship"
1. A written statement of faith affirming their evangelical commitment.

2. A board which meets at least twice a year. A majority of the board members must not be employees, staff, or relatives of employees or staff. This reduces conflicts of interest.

3. Annual auditing by an independent accounting firm.

4. An audit review committee appointed by the board (half must be outsiders) which reviews the annual audit and reports its findings to the board.

5. Current audited statements given to anyone upon written request.

6. Activities conducted with the highest standards of integrity.

7. Fund-raising appeals which clearly identify the purpose and programs for which the donations will be used.

If your movement has not established guidelines of this type, either the General Secretary or board chairman ought to take the initiative in calling for a financial policies review.

Even in local churches it is wise to have safeguards. For example, in Leadership magazine, winter 1987, Rev. Ed Hales says that in his church "We require that a minimum of three people do the counting, in the same room at the same time. When the envelope is opened, the counters verify that the amount shown on the front of the envelope matches what's in it. If it doesn't, the correct figure is marked on the envelope with a felt pen. The envelope then becomes the means of recording." [And safeguards false accusations by donors in the event the donation is in cash and the donor forgets the amount given that Sunday.]

Rev. Hales goes on to say, "We also break the chain in as many places as possible so the persons who receive, count, and deposit the money are never permitted to spend it. And at the advice of our accountant, we no longer allow the financial secretary or the treasurer to reconcile our bank statement. That's being done by the auditing committee."

Although we may not often receive cash, these careful

procedures are desirable even when payments come in the form of checks.

Formal receipts are a vital link in the chain of safeguards, and should be kept in safekeeping so that only authorized individuals issue them.

By now I hope even the newly-established movements realize that accounting is an important part of an orderly Christian ministry. As Paul writes to the Corinthians (I Cor. 14:40) "everything should be done in a fitting and orderly way." Money matters are a part of the "everything."

20
FUND RAISING I

Board/council members and staff often find themselves talking about how to provide adequate funds for the work to be done in the movement. This is usually a necessary, but distasteful, subject. Why?

Most staff workers have been attracted to student ministry because they love students and want to spend time telling them about Christ and then teaching them how to become His disciples. They have been encouraged to become staff workers because God has given them gifts as evangelizers and disciplers while they were undergraduates themselves.

But fund raising is unpalatable. The very idea of asking someone for money repels them. It is at the unsavory end of their preferences, an unseemly task for a student worker.

Fortunately, there are some talented student workers who are both gifted in fund raising and enjoy it. But some of our finest workers seem neither gifted nor inclined toward fund raising.

What is the answer?

Let's go back to the beginning. When a student movement comes into being, one of its commitments is to be self-supporting, since each national movement within IFES is expected to find within its own nation the resources to fund its ministry.

At this early stage, much of the work is done by volunteers who are either board/council members or campus workers, or both. Very little money is required to keep the ministry thriving.

As the ministry grows, however, the over-worked volunteers agree that some full-time employees are needed for campus and office tasks. This need thrusts the movement into a new situation. The leaders are forced to discover a means whereby these workers and their expenses can be paid. In doing so, they must answer questions such as the following:

Questions to Answer
* Where is the money going to come from?
* What place does prayer have in fund raising?
* How are we going to contact those whom we expect to give?
* Should the board/council assume full responsibility for fund raising?
* What part should the staff play in raising funds for their work?
* What expenses, if any, should be paid by the students who are receiving help?
* Should we expect graduates of our work to underwrite the entire budget?
* What portion of the effort should be carried out by the national office? By the regional, area or local staff or committees?

1. How Do We Go About Answering All of These Questions?
Although we haven't space to comment on all of them now, let's try to understand some basic issues surrounding them.

Fortunately, a movement sometimes has leisure to answer them one by one over a period of time. If growth is slow and steady, a few board/council members may be able to speak to a couple of friends, or staff may be able to ap-

proach a few graduates. The small amount needed is readily made up.

Eventually, however, all of the above questions will require an answer. And it is wisest if THE BOARD/ COUNCIL AND SEVERAL OF THE SENIOR STAFF WORKERS OR VOLUNTEERS WORK TOGETHER in resolving these questions. Why? Since both groups will need to be involved in the work of fund raising.

Oh, I do remember in the early days of IVCF-USA our General Secretary, Stacey Woods, told the few of us on staff not to worry about fund raising. He and Mr. Petersen, the Stewardship Secretary, would handle that with the monthly letter they sent out to friends and churches. He told us that our job was to work on campus, and we were to devote all our energies there.

But in the years that followed, the vision outgrew the resources of those monthly letters, and campus workers were enlisted in the fund-raising aspect of the movement.

And that is where many of our movements find themselves today: holding a great vision which is going to demand far greater financial resources than their present sources can provide. We are like Joshua standing on the edge of Jordan with a task far greater than human means alone can accomplish.

2. What Resources are Available to a Movement?

a. As a foundation to all other resources, each movement has the PROMISES OF GOD'S WORD to undergird all they do. Such promises range from the all-important promise of His presence (which He gave to Moses, as well as the early disciples) to Paul's word to the Philippians, "My God will meet all your needs according to His glorious riches in Christ Jesus." These good words of encouragement nurture our faith and confidence in days when the task seems too lonely, the vision too great.

b. We also have the LEGACY OF THE HOLY SPIRIT'S WORK in the lives of students and others who have been influenced by the movement. As GRADUATES, many of us know from personal experience that we are still involved with the student movement because God worked mightily in our lives when we were in a student union. Even a significant part of our benevolence giving is shared with a vision and prayer that others' lives may be changed through the movement, even as ours was.

c. Talented STAFF MEMBERS AND COMMITTED BOARD/COUNCIL PEOPLE form the prime resource team. Each one has a unique contribution to make if we will use creativity in harnessing his/her abilities.

d. The entire BODY OF CHRIST in the Church everywhere is joined with us in the student ministry. Even though parts of the Body of Christ are engaged in different ministries, we are all ONE in Christ Jesus. And this means that every body of believers is potentially inclined positively toward sharing in our work among students. Ours is not a work confined to an exclusive few. Those who have found Christ through IFES movements are members of many church denominations. They are serving in every sector of Christian ministry today: among children and the aging, the destitute and affluent, the urban minorities and the tribal peoples of many continents. Some graduates are in high government positions, others in social service agencies among the urban squatters. IFES is truly serving the entire body of Christ.

3. Now back to our initial question:
Where is the money going to come from?
Begin with those who are:
* already interested,
* easiest to reach,
* most likely to contribute.

Who will these customarily be?

* graduates who were helped and active in the movement
* board/committee people who are or were active participants
* parents of graduates, staff, and students who are Christians themselves
* members of home and campus churches of staff, students, and committee people
* churches which share the evangelical vision of IFES.

In some countries TRUSTS or FOUNDATIONS are established in order to distribute earnings or contributed funds to worthy recipients. Most of us in IFES have heard of TEAR fund (Great Britain) or World Vision (mainly USA) which give generously to ministries around the world. Many other organizations exist in various countries which may be ready to contribute to a national movement. It is worth investigating these sources in your own nation to determine which may be committed to helping a work such as yours. Each foundation or trust will have a statement which defines the kinds of ministry it will fund. Exploring these options is worthwhile, since such organizations will often continue grants over a number of years.

In rare cases, GOVERNMENT SUBSIDIES are available to agencies that engage in youth ministry. Where this has been available without control of activities or message, it has been of great help.

STUDENTS assist in fund raising as well, through prayer, personal donations, work projects (car washes, etc.), and making needs known to friends and family.

4. Now we face the question,
What place does prayer have in fund-raising?
We must go no further without recognizing that in mission circles there are those who feel that PRAYER

ALONE is the ideal means of raising whatever money is required to carry on the Lord's work. George Muller of the well-known orphan homes in Bristol, England, and J. Hudson Taylor of the China Inland Mission founded ministries that not only survived, but thrived and grew through dependence upon God through prayer alone.

In a book published by Overseas Missionary Fellowship in 1990, Roger Steer has selected quotations from George Muller which confirm that Muller's main aim was to quicken faith in God. On page 16 of A LIVING REALITY (titled SPIRITUAL SECRETS OF GEORGE MULLER by OMF and Shaw publishers in USA) Steer quotes Muller:

"Now if I, a poor man simply by prayer and faith, obtained, without asking any individual, the means for establishing and carrying on an orphan-house: there would be something which, with the Lord's blessing, might be instrumental in strengthening the faith of the children of God, besides being a testimony to the consciences of the unconverted of the reality of the things of God.

Muller wrote that God's promises in Matthew 7:7-8; John 14:13-14; and Matthew 6:25-34 "were the stay of my soul."

The Overseas Missionary Fellowship (the present name of China Inland Mission), which today has more than 900 workers, has continued to follow this principle for more than 120 years. This mission informs people about its ministry through periodicals, letters, audio-visuals and mission deputation. But no worker is allowed to ask for money. They may answer questions raised by churches and individuals about support needs, but never take initiative except in prayer.

Now let's ask the question again: How do we get in touch with potential donors? Will we simply tell them about the work, like Muller and Taylor, or will we make our needs known, as the Apostle Paul did? Re-read chapters 8 and 9 of 2 Corinthians as one example of the

Apostle's approach. If your leadership team is uncertain about the propriety of publicly expressing needs, open discussion in the context of Bible study is an appropriate way to begin to come to a united understanding of God's way for your movement. If your stated purpose is to prove that God answers prayer, the Muller approach may be right.

No matter which course of action we take, the same fundamental principle applies: we must TRUST GOD to supply our needs, rather than relying on our persuasive powers, our asking, our letters, the number of prayers, our own holiness, the worthiness of our work, or whatever programs we may develop.

What are some of the indications that we are trusting God?

1. We will pray (both individually and together) before, during and after we have done all we know to do.
2. We will thank God, even as we thank those whom He leads to give.
3. We will be joyful people as we wait for His provision, knowing that He who hears in secret will reward us openly.

IFES International and most of our movements have been led to follow the pattern of the Apostle Paul: they openly express their needs to people, churches and agencies that share a concern for evangelizing and discipling students. At the same time they aim to trust God as the One who is moving in the hearts and minds and circumstances of people so the needs are met. This is the context for the ideas shared below.

5. What Means Should We Use to Share Our Needs?

Here is a partial list of the most popular means:
1. Letters. Advantages are: easy to prepare, everyone gets

the same message, prayer requests can be stated clearly, reply envelopes may be included, and letters are comparatively inexpensive. Weaknesses are their lack of interaction and a declining level of interest if no face-to-face contact occurs year after year.

2. Face-to-face visit. This is by far the best means available, since it can be personalized, interactive (you can answer questions and tailor-make the presentation to each person). The main problem is the time it requires, both to set up the appointment, to travel, and then to actually interact with the person.

3. Telephone conversation. This gives voice contact, is personalized, allows for interaction, saves travel time. Problems occur when people are away from home a lot, or they have no phones in their homes, or if the telephone system is unreliable. Some people do not communicate well on the telephone, so the contact is less effective than other means.

4. Group meetings. Church services, youth groups, church school classes, and various club meetings save time for the speaker, but lack the personal quality of individual encounters. This weakness is often overcome by personal talks after group meetings, and it gives a chance to meet people whom you would otherwise have no chance to contact.

5. Group events you sponsor. One of the best ways to communicate with several people at once is to invite them to participate in a conference, or to attend a meeting where they can observe your ministry in action, or to a special gathering where you report on what God is doing among students. In some countries an annual or periodic "banquet" is a congenial setting for reporting to interested friends. In 1988 the Canadian IVCF used the occasion of its 60th anniversary to communicate God's faithfulness by sponsoring a banquet, as did the Jamaican movement for its 40th birthday. Celebration is a joyous setting for building rapport with old and new friends. Much work is involved,

but it is also a fine occasion to use volunteers and strengthen ties with them. Several movements have worked out a kind of handbook for those responsible for banquets, since larger movements may sponsor several each year.

6. Illustrated news letter. An adaptation of the letter is a PERIODIC NEWS SHEET which contains articles about student and staff activities, photos of people, places and events, information about financial needs, and a calendar of events ahead. All of these can stimulate prayer, good will, and financial support. IFES international's annual "Overview" served this purpose well for several years. A small movement may wish to begin with a more modest "quickprint" format, which would be easier and less costly. But it is usually wiser to keep it attractive, and produce a fine semi-annual edition, rather than a careless, unattractive monthly.

Many Questions Remain. In other chapters we discuss the place of staff in fund raising, as well as the division of responsibility between central and local support.

21
FUND-RAISING II

Who Should Do the Fund-Raising?

This question has no fixed answer, since a movement is a dynamic, changing entity. What may be right at one point in history may be inadequate later. Consequently, the leaders of a movement must make a decision before a severe financial crisis leads to bankruptcy.

The two extremes between which movements fluctuate range from a) placing the complete burden on the staff to b) using volunteers and board/committee members to release the full energies of the staff for student work.

Those organizations that place the full burden on the staff do not allow a person to begin campus ministry until his/her full support is given or pledged. Those movements that spread responsibility combine the efforts of board/council, staff, regional or local volunteer committees, and central support people to insure that each person's needs are met. One other common approach is to publicize the total annual budget, work together in making the need known, pool all income, and then share the provision according to previously agreed guidelines.

THE EASY WAY. A board/council and general secretary throw off most of the fund-raising burden when they require staff to raise their own support before they begin employment with the movement.

By defining "support" as salary, travel, phone and office expense, pension, health insurance, social security, and a proportion of central office expense, the leaders are able to throw off most of the burden of fund-raising. The total amount thus becomes about twice as much as the person's

salary, making this approach ANYTHING BUT EASY for
the staff.

Mission societies in USA that use this approach find that
candidates spend from 18 to 24 months raising support
before going overseas or beginning language study.

THE EASY WAY RECONSIDERED. Before adopting the
easy way, consider the following hazards:

1. LOSS OF CANDIDATES. Some gifted potential student
workers find the idea of raising a large amount of money
so distasteful or overwhelming that they don't seriously
consider applying.

2. FAILURE. Certain gifted candidates may fail to raise the
required amount of support and thus be unable to join the
team.   They may be gifted in ministry, but not in fund
raising. Or they may be located in an area where available
support is inadequate.

3. STUDENT MINISTRY IS HAMPERED.

Those who do succeed in getting their support will find
that fund-raising diverts their attention and consumes great
amounts of time. Preoccupation with financial shortages
can prove demoralizing. At least annually, and often at
more frequent intervals, financial shortages require staff to
spend large blocks of time in fund raising, rather than
student ministry. The need to maintain frequent contact
with donors will often take priority over the student
unions. And sometimes crucial periods for ministry in the
academic year coincide with the financial crises, so that
students don't receive the help they need.

4. MONEY BECOMES DECISIVE. When a person applying
for staff has strong fund-raising potential, it is tempting to
accept him, even though his ministry skills are weak. Staff
leaders sometimes weaken their teams by making success
in fund-raising the prime criterion in choosing potential
staff.

5. STAFF TURNOVER IS COSTLY. When individuals raise their own support, they customarily appeal to people and churches who are primarily interested in them personally, rather than in their schools and students. Thus when they leave staff, their successors must re-raise their entire support.

6. A BETTER WAY. Rather than leaving fund raising to any individual, it is appropriate that everyone share in the task. Fund raising can be a unifying influence when the gifts of everyone are wisely combined to do the work.

The Apostle Paul points out that we are one body in Christ, and in 1 Corinthians 12:24 tells us that "God has combined the members of the body . . . so that there should be no division in the body, but that its parts should have equal concern for each other." Bearing in mind this principle, some will be gifted in one aspect of fund raising, while others may be gifted in another. Prayer, sharing what God is doing, telling new people about the work, writing thank-you letters, telephoning, keeping names, addresses and phone numbers up-to-date, counting pledges, and many other functions are all needed.

Working alone in fund-raising is wearisome; joining others a joy.

Consider These Principles

1. In the legal documents which establish the movement, the board/council is given full responsibility for the financial health of the movement. Even though others may carry out most aspects of fund-raising, the basic responsibility for insuring that all financial obligations are met cannot be avoided.

2. The continued existence of the organization depends upon receiving sufficient funds to pay all obligations incurred by the movement. No more can be spent than is received.

3. The board/council may delegate to employees of the organization both the fund-raising function and the control of expenses. In this case the board/council may use ANNUAL income and expense budget approval as well as INTERMEDIATE financial checkpoints to fulfill its fiscal responsibility.

4. The board/council will determine OVERALL POLICIES that define the role that employees of the organization will have in fund raising. For example, if a movement has outgrown the resources of board members and their own immediate circle of contacts, they will need to locate others to assist by either 1) finding some volunteers who will form local or area committees that accept fund-raising tasks, or 2) guide the General Secretary in assigning fund-raising activities to employees. Various employees may be assigned to recruit volunteers or engage in any other aspect of fund-raising.

5. If the movement uses employees to establish local fund-raising committees, it is important for any board/council members of these committees to remember that the employee takes his orders from the General Secretary. Otherwise an employee could be caught between two bosses.

6. Fund-raising activities necessarily divert staff energy from student ministry. Student ministry expectations need to be scaled back to allow for the careful planning and large amounts of time which fund raising entails. The same is true for office employees who raise support.

How Do We Go About Dividing Up the Work?

Initially, a representative group of board/council and staff (preferably 3 to 8 people) should work with the General Secretary in making a "wish" list of tasks which, ideally, should be done.

Such a list might include entries such as the following:

A. CONTACTING PRESENT SUPPORTERS.

    1. Writing a monthly newsletter.

    2. Producing and mailing the newsletter.

    3. Keeping the list up-to-date.

    4. Receiving donations, keeping financial records, and sending receipts and thank-you notes to donors.

    5. Tabulating responses, and on a regular basis informing staff and committees about these responses.

    6. Planning special events so donors, students and staff can share face-to-face what God is doing.

    7. Preparing each month a list of prayer requests and answers to be sent to present supporters. These may be combined with the newsletter.

B. FINDING NEW SUPPORTERS.

    1. Deciding where potential new supporters are most likely to be found.

    2. Thinking through which means are going to be best to contact these potential supporters.

    3. Developing an annual calendar to designate what will be done each month.

    4. Finding volunteers to do many of the jobs listed on the annual calendar.

    5. Coordinating the work of the volunteers and carrying out the plans.

C. GENERAL PUBLICITY.

    1. Deciding how to make the movement known in the larger Christian community, utilizing such means as newspapers, magazines, radio, and television.

    2. Making an annual calendar describing how publicity will be timed throughout the year ahead.

3. Finding volunteers and assigning tasks to both employees and volunteers who will carry out the annual publicity plan.

Once the "wish" list is fairly clear, leaders must focus on the available resources. It is tempting to expect busy employees or board/council members to carry out the plans once they have been made. Furthermore, it is tempting to count on the extra income generated by these plans to cover the costs of carrying them out. NEITHER ASSUMP-TION IS SAFE.

The most difficult task in dividing up the work is convert-ing your "wish" list into a realistic plan for the year. Both the human and financial resources need to be realistically assessed.

How Do We Assess Our Resources?

Do we simply let the people who've made up the "wish" list work back from this ideal to a realistic approach?

That might seem easy, but it is unrealistic in two ways: (1) Those making the assessment will rarely have at their fingertips any clear idea of the present work load of staff and volunteers; and (2) those who will carry out the task may not necessarily agree with or understand what needs to be done if they are simply handed a decision.

A better way is to bring into the decision-making process at this point those staff and volunteer coordinators who will be involved. Their input will be invaluable in keeping this aspect of fund-raising realistic. And it will greatly boost their morale.

Furthermore, the cost of carrying out the plans must be assessed and built into the budget for the following year. Even though volunteers may not require salary, the work they do will cost money for printing, postage, telephone, and travel. Those familiar with the ebb and flow of income to the movement need to be brought in at this point, if they are not already involved.

No program will work without planning expenses in advance. Neither will it work without an agreement, in advance, as to who is responsible to raise each part of the budget. Time guidelines are a useful part of this whole exercise, and will help fund raisers schedule their work and at the same time avoid financial crises which are painful to everyone. MONTHLY REPORTS of both money received and money spent are helpful to all who are involved in praying and working together. A MEETING EVERY THREE MONTHS to review progress and make appropriate adjustments is invaluable.

Temptations for Fund-Raisers

1. DISTORTING TRUTH . . . in order to gain the attention, sympathy, gifts and prayers of people. By inflating the positive signs of God's work, or by pronouncing impending doom if gifts are not received, the fund raiser tries to increase and/or hasten the donor's response. This is often called MANIPULATION, which is defined as "to adapt or change (accounts, figures, etc.) to suit one's purpose or advantage."

2. DELAYING ACTION . . . until there are no reserves left or a financial crisis point is imminent. The needs of individual students and student leaders often clamor for our attention. But donors are passive and require the fund raiser to initiate contact. So until a financial shortage threatens the student ministry, fund raising is given low priority.

3. DEPENDING ON EMOTION . . . instead of information. Although people may give a single donation in response to an urgent appeal for help, their long-term gifts will come to the student movement as they hear how God is transforming the lives of students.

Crisis appeals soon lose their effectiveness as people begin to question the leadership of a movement that lives on the edge of bankruptcy.

4. FOCUSING ON MONEY . . . instead of on the vision of God's call. It is easy to write an entire letter describing the financial aspects of the work and the immediate problems caused by lack of funds. The great challenge of students without Christ may be forgotten.

5. "OWNING" DONORS . . . so that I resent their giving to any other work. Even as the Lord has led someone to give money to our work, so He may lead them to give to others.

6. FORGETTING THE PERSON . . . in the same way that some salespeople relate to people only as potential customers. It is easy to forget that each donor is a fellow Christian who has hopes and fears, joys and sorrows like us. Whether or not they give a donation, they deserve our love and care. We owe them more than a sales pitch.